# Essays on Manuscripts and Rare Books

1. Fragment of St. Gregory's *Moralia in Job*
Beinecke Rare Book and Manuscript Library, Yale University MS 516

# *Essays on*

# MANUSCRIPTS AND RARE BOOKS

BY

Cora E. Lutz

ARCHON BOOKS

1975

*Library of Congress Cataloging in Publication Data*

Lutz, Cora Elizabeth
Essays on manuscripts and rare books.

Includes bibliographical references and index.
CONTENTS: Early manuscript fragments: A manuscript fragment from Bede's Monastery. A manuscript of
Charlemagne's Homiliarium. A bifolium from the Sacramentarium Gregorianum. [etc.]
1. Manuscripts, Latin—History—Addresses, essays,
lectures. 2. Bibliography—Rare books—History—Addresses, essays, lectures. 3. Literature, Medieval—History
and criticism—Addresses, essays, lectures. I. Title.
Z6602.L87                       091                       75-2323
ISBN 0-208-01513-2

© 1975 by Cora E. Lutz
First published 1975 as an Archon Book
an imprint of The Shoe String Press, Inc.,
Hamden, Connecticut 06514

*Printed in the United States of America*

*To Mary E. Knapp*

# CONTENTS

## ILLUSTRATIONS

# PREFACE

The unread book has always evoked an emotional response from bibliophiles. This can be illustrated by three examples. In a colophon to one of the manuscripts of his *Synonyma de homine et ratione*, written in the seventh century, Isidore of Seville makes an earnest plea. He asks that the person into whose hands the book may come will read it often and entrust it to others to be copied so that it may be used as widely as possible. He expresses great regret that there are many who acquire books that are handsome and beautifully bound, but they keep them locked up in cases, without reading them themselves or permitting others to do so, unaware that such books are useless. Poggio-Bracciolini, in a letter to Guarino, dated at Constance in 1417, vividly describes his dual feelings of anger and exultation when, in his search for manuscripts at the monastery of St. Gall, at the bottom of a dank, disused tower he came upon a volume of Quintilian that had been lying for centuries in the grime and dust, almost lost forever. At the end of the fifteenth century Sebastian Brant in his *Ship of Fools* mockingly gives first place among the passengers to the bibliomaniac who thus condemns himself:

In dunce's dance I take the lead,
Books useless, numerous my creed,
Which I can't understand or read.

At the present time when most books are generally available, only some rare books are unread because they are not easily accessible. Even in this field, however, the situation has greatly improved since many large private book collections have been dispersed and, for the most part, the books are now in institutional libraries. More important, in this country in the last three decades the great university libraries have taken their precious manuscripts and rare books from improvised and often inconvenient storage spaces and provided separate libraries where they are both secure and readily available to scholars.

While cataloguing the Medieval and Renaissance manuscripts in the Beinecke Rare Book and Manuscript Library of Yale University, I have had the opportunity to read many unusual and some unique manuscripts and early books that have claimed my attention. Some of the special questions they have raised I have treated in these essays.

Many of the essays have been printed in the *Yale University Library Gazette*, and I am grateful to the editor, Donald Gallup, for permitting me to reprint them here. For similar permission for one that was originally printed in the *Harvard Library Bulletin*, I wish to thank the editor, Edwin L. Williams. Likewise I wish to express my appreciation to Elizabeth Story Donno, editor of the *Renaissance Quarterly,* for the privilege of reprinting the essay on the Martianus Capella commentary. I am indebted to the Beinecke Library of Yale, the Houghton Library of Harvard, the Bibliothèque nationale, and the Sächsische Landesbibliothek of Dresden for allowing me to reproduce illustrations from manuscripts or rare books from their libraries.

Most of my research was carried on in the Sterling Library and the Beinecke Library of Yale University. It gives me deep satisfaction to have an opportunity to thank the librarians and staffs of both these great libraries for their innumerable kindnesses and their unfailing cooperation in advancing my work. My special thanks go to Marjorie G. Wynne, Research Librarian at Beinecke Library. I should also like to express my gratitude to Carolyn E. Jakeman of the Houghton Library of Harvard for all the assistance she has provided me.

C. E. L.

New Haven, Connecticut

*He who passes much of his time amid such vast resources, and does not aspire to make some small addition to his library, were it only by a critical catalogue, must indeed be not more animated than a leaden Mercury.*

I. Disraeli, *Curiosities of Literature*

*Part I*

Early Manuscript Fragments

# A Manuscript Fragment
## from Bede's Monastery

The best known anecdote in the Venerable Bede's *Ecclesiastical History of the English Nation* is without question the story of St. Gregory's introduction to the natives of the island of Britain about the year 574. When as a young monk he saw some fair-haired, angelic-faced boys put up for sale in a slave market in Rome and learned that they were Angli, he determined to make it his personal mission to convert those splendid people to Christianity. Having obtained the reluctant consent of the Pope, Gregory set out for Britain, but on the fourth day was summoned back to Rome. The rest of his life was so crowded with ecclesiastical responsibilities that he never found an opportunity even to visit the land of the Angli. When he himself became Pope in 596, however, one of his first acts was to send Augustine and forty other monks to take the Gospel to Britain. Pursuing this objective with great vigor throughout his reign, keeping ever in close touch with his emissaries, exhorting and advising them by letter, he finally had the satisfaction of learning of the conversion of King Ethelbert in 602. Although unofficially Gregory has usually been designated the apostle to the English, it is significant that the epitaph on his tomb records as the most notable achievement of this great Father of the Church that "Ad Christum Anglos convertit."[1]

One very important result of Augustine's mission was the founding of monasteries, especially the sister houses of St. Peter at Wearmouth and St. Paul at Jarrow, where the Venerable Bede received his religious training and his education in the liberal arts. Bede relates that in the scriptorium of these monasteries, about the year 700, the learned Abbot Ceolfrid had three copies of the Vulgate made, one for each of the monasteries and the third for a gift to the Pope. The abbot himself set out for Rome in 716 to make the presentation. Unfortunately, he died when he reached Langres; but his followers apparently carried out his wishes and gave the book to Pope Gregory II.[2] The wanderings of that Bible thereafter are known only in part: about 900 it was given to the monastery of S. Salvatore at Monte Amiata. Upon the disestablishment of that monastery in 1782, it went to the Laurentian Library in Florence where, designated the Codex Amiatinus,[3] it is now one of the foremost treasures of that great library. Along with the Lindisfarne Gospels and the Book of Kells, it is commonly considered one of the most beautiful books in the western world.

Of the other two copies of the Vulgate prepared under the supervision of Ceolfrid, just eleven separate folios have survived the ravages that England suffered at the hands of numerous invaders.[4] From the same scriptorium where numerous other works must have been copied, only a few fragments have now been identified in several libraries of Europe.[5] By a happy chance, one such fragment has recently come to the Beinecke Library and is now listed as MS 516. By an equally fortunate chance, the text of the Yale fragment is a part of the *Moralia in Job*, one of the most ambitious of the writings of that same Gregory I who was responsible for introducing Christianity into Britain.

It is impossible to guess what vicissitudes overtook the original manuscript; this lone fragment may have been preserved only because it had been used at one time in the binding of a book. It must have traveled to the Continent before the fourteenth century, for in one corner it bears an inscription of ownership: "Liber iste est fratris Reyneri de Capella. Orate pro eo." Reynerus, a bibliophile monk, has left similar inscriptions on several other manuscripts. It is known that he lived at a Benedictine monastery at Soest in Westphalia in the fourteenth century.[6] Since then, presumably, the manuscript has remained in Germany.

The Yale fragment is only the upper half of the original folio leaf of heavy vellum. Its size now, after having been trimmed on three sides, is 172 by 235 millimeters. The rather large letters are written in a single column. The script is a graceful, firm, precise English uncial hand very similar to, if not identical with, that of the Codex Amiatinus. The ink is dark and clear; there are no erasures or corrections, but in three instances a second hand has supplied several letters missing at the end of a line. As an example of beautiful calligraphy it has few rivals anywhere. This is all the more remarkable for the fact that it is one of the very earliest manuscripts produced in Britain.

The portion of the text of the *Moralia* that is preserved in the manuscript is from the eighteenth book, chapters 41 and 42, where St. Gregory is expounding the text of the Book of Job at the beginning of chapter 28 (*Patrologia Latina,* LXXVI.59). In this chapter, which is a profound poem on man's quest for wisdom, a striking contrast is drawn between man's skill in discovering, mining, and refining precious metals and his complete inability to find wisdom, which can only come by the grace of God. In his commentary, Gregory endeavors to explain the text literally, then to show its spiritual meaning, and finally to apply it to the lives of his readers. Unfortunately our brief text touches only the first verse of the chapter, and even then there is a hiatus, because the lower half of the folio is missing. At any rate, Gregory considers the first verse a parable of the universal Church and its relation to heretics and schismatics. As gold is refined by fire, the true Christian passing through the furnace of

suffering has his sins purged away, but the heretic is burned
by the fire and he is not purified, just as Jeremiah foretold
(VI:29). Those who divide the Church and hence show no
love for their brothers are also burned because they are bereft
of the gift of grace; as St. Paul says, "Though I give my body
to be burned, and have not charity, it profiteth me nothing"
(I Corinthians XIII:3).

The Latin text, too, is of interest because it represents a
very early recension. Although there are many manuscripts
that preserve the text of Gregory's *Moralia*, not one is older
than our fragment.[7] In only three instances a word of the
text in the fragment differs slightly in spelling from the
modern edition of Gregory. It is also worthy of note that
in two cases where the same quotation from Paul's *Letter
to the Corinthians* is given, the text has a word that occurs
in the old Itala version of the Bible rather than that of
Jerome's Vulgate edition, normally used in Gregory's time.[8]

Beyond these considerations, the fragment makes an appeal
to sentiment, especially at this time. When the ecclesiastical
world is commemorating the thirteenth centenary of the
birth of the Venerable Bede, "the Father of English History,"
it is tempting to seek an association of Bede with this manuscript fragment. Among the books that Benedict Biscop,
the founder of the monasteries of Wearmouth and Jarrow,
brought back from his six journeys to Italy between 653
and 683 were the *Moralia* and other works of St. Gregory.
Bede, who was brought to Wearmouth at the age of seven
and remained at the twin monasteries his entire life, must
have studied these works when he was a pupil of Ceolfrid
and then in turn used them himself to teach succeeding
generations of monks. In all of his writings, but particularly
in his commentaries on the Bible, Bede quotes freely from
the *Moralia*. He developed a deep veneration not only for
Gregory's works but for his life. In his *Ecclesiastical History*
Bede preserved some of Gregory's letters that deal with the
conversion of the English, and his account of the death of
Gregory is a very moving tribute to his spiritual father. It

is not difficult, then, to imagine that when the monastery's most talented copyist prepared the large and splendid volume of the *Moralia,* Bede must have admired the workmanship and turned the pages reverently and carefully. Now, only one folio, the Yale fragment, is known to have survived from that beautiful book which may have been used by the saintly scholar Bede, whom St. Boniface called "a candle lighted by the Holy Spirit."[9]

# A Manuscript

## of Charlemagne's *Homiliarium*

Following the example of his father, Pippin, who had reformed the services of the Church in introducing the Gregorian chant into the liturgy of the Frankish churches, Charlemagne took steps to improve the preaching by eliminating the faulty and inadequate sermons in common use and by procuring a supply of correct and appropriate homilies. To accomplish this he enlisted the aid of Paulus Diaconus, the learned scholar and Benedictine monk of Monte Cassino. With the cooperation of Abbot Benedict, Paulus went through the works of the Church Fathers and selected the best sermons and tracts he could find. These he arranged, along with suitable Gospel readings, to extend through the liturgical year. The emperor, after approving the work, directed an unusual *Epistola generalis*,[1] in which he recommended the regular use of this official book of homilies to the bishops throughout his wide realm.

The *Homiliarium* was such a large work that it was normally divided into two volumes. The first, called *Pars hiemalis*,

contained Gospel readings and sermons for all the Sundays
and feast days from the first Sunday in Advent to Holy Saturday; the second, *Pars aestivalis,* continued from Easter Sunday
to Advent. The sermons were taken from the works of Bede,
St. Augustine, St. Jerome, St. Gregory, St. Maximus of Turin,
Pope Leo, Isidore of Seville, Fulgentius, St. John Chrysostom,
St. Caesarius, and others.

After Charlemagne's letter to the bishops, which was sent
out about 797, a great many copies of the *Homiliarium* must
have been made to supply the churches. Yet, of those early
manuscripts, from the ninth and tenth centuries, only six,
either complete or nearly so, have survived. Perhaps a score
more, many incomplete, some very fragmentary, represent
copies made in later times. These manuscripts are now in
libraries in Germany, Switzerland, Holland, France, Italy,
and England.[2] In the United States only one manuscript,
a twelfth-century copy of twenty-three leaves, has been re-
ported (in the University of Illinois Library).[3] The *Homiliarium* was printed by six publishers in Germany and Switzerland before 1500. Of these incunabula, Yale has a copy of the
edition printed in Nuremberg by Anton Koberger in 1494.
The only modern text is in Migne's *Patrologia Latina* (XCV,
1160-1566).

Recently a manuscript in the Beinecke Library has been
identified as part of Paulus Diaconus' *Homiliarium.* This
manuscript (MS 151 of the Marston collection), written about
A. D. 900, is composed of sixty-one leaves of heavy vellum with
the text written in two columns of twenty-nine lines in the
characteristic Carolingian minuscule script. It must have
received hard usage, for it is well-worn, yellowed, sewn and
patched in places, with the lower corners of the leaves limp
from frequent turning. The first two folios are missing, as
is the last one. It would seem originally to have contained
the first part of the *Pars hiemalis,* for the text begins in the
middle of Bede's sermon for Wednesday of the week before
Christmas and ends just before Epiphany, with twenty-eight
sermons in all. The Gospel readings are identified, but the

only sermon which is credited to its author is the first one by Bede. There are no corrections or marginal notes, but on a few folios a number of letters have been re-inked. Some nineteenth-century reader has written in identifications (a few incorrect) of the authors.

Little is known of the history of the manuscript. Very likely it was copied in some monastery in France. At an undetermined date it came into the possession of the Cistercian abbey which had been founded at Hautecombe near Lake Geneva in 1121. When the abbey was disestablished in 1792, the volume was obtained along with eleven other manuscripts by the Seminario Metropolitano of Turin. There and then the book may have lost some clues as to its history, for Monseigneur Hyacinthe della Torre had all twelve manuscripts uniformly rebound and did not preserve the original flyleaves and covers. In 1957 the Turin Seminario sold its valuable manuscripts to an American bookseller. The *Homiliarium* was then purchased by Thomas E. Marston, and it came to Yale when the Library obtained the Marston collection in 1961.

Scholars who have studied the *Homiliarium* have directed their attention to solving two problems: (1) the original content of the book, and (2) the original text. As one might expect, during the course of the years additional sermons came to be included as one church or another sought to honor some local saint, and the later manuscripts present considerable variations in content. Happily, the first problem was solved when Dom Leclercq, after examining the earliest of the manuscripts, published in 1948 a list of two hundred and forty-four authentic homilies.[4]

The original text, however, remains to be established. The only modern printed text, that in the *Patrologia*, was based, unfortunately, on an early edition printed in Cologne in 1539. Since this was prepared before currently accepted principles of textual criticism had been laid down, it does not succeed in giving an adequate representation of the original text. The task for the modern editor will be to examine all the manuscripts, but particularly the earliest, to determine what

the original must have been. For this, naturally, the ninth-
and tenth-century manuscripts will be of great importance,
and one hopes that Yale Marston MS 151 will be found
especially reliable.

# A Bifolium from a
## *Sacramentarium Gregorianum*

Terentianus Maurus' frequently quoted aphorism, "Books, too, have their destinies," seems to apply with particular poignancy to handwritten books. During the Middle Ages, apart from the uncounted thousands of manuscripts that perished through the ravages of war, in conflagrations, or through ignorance and neglect, a large group of books was destroyed purposely, often in the very monasteries where they were kept. When a parchment manuscript was no longer wanted, either because the text was obsolete, or the book was damaged, or conditions within the monastery had changed so that it was no longer needed, there were two options: (1) to put it aside, or (2) to reuse it. Since vellum was not only expensive and sometimes hard to find but so durable that it could be expected to last indefinitely, the second alternative was most often taken. In many cases a large, unwieldy old book was divided to provide material to make smaller ones; the old writing was scraped off, the surface polished, and a new text was inscribed. Now that a means of restoring the original has been devised,

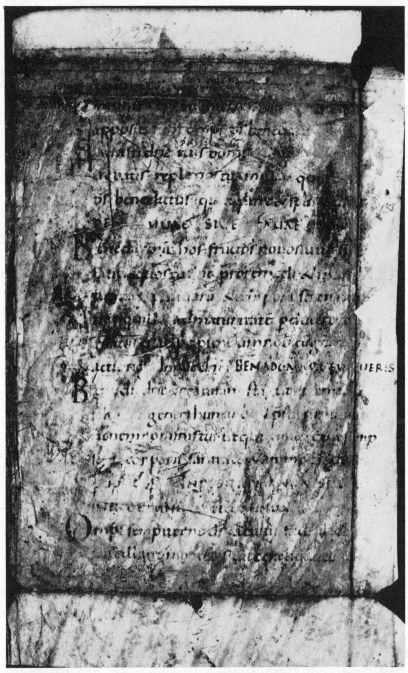

2. Bifolium from a *Sacramentarium Gregorianum*
Beinecke Rare Book and Manuscript Library, Yale University MS 484 no. 6

possideri · sed potius tenera etas maligni

oppressionib; liberata · tibi referat gras

sempiternas· p dnm nrm ihm xpm filiu tuu ·

qui uenturus e iudicare uiuos &mortuos

&sctm igne· p          ALIA OR SUPER

INERGUMINUM BAPTIZATO

O r sanctoy · & archangeloy · & pphary · or

uctoy · & martyrum · & uirginu · & pa

ter dni nri ihu xpi · inuoco nomen sctm tuum

ac p clarem maiestatis tue clementia supplex

exposco ut mihi auxilium p stare digneris

aduersus hunc nequissimum spm · ut ubi

cumq; latet audito nomine tuo uelociter

exeat ut recedat; Ipse tibi imperat diabole ·

qui uentis & mari · ut tempestatibus imperauit ·

Ipse tibi imperat·qui te de supnis celoru in in

feriora terre demergi p cepit · Ipse tibi im

perat qui te retror sum redire p cepit; audi

ergo et time satanas·uictus & prostratus

abscede · in nomine dni nri ihu xpi ; tu ergo

nequissime satanas: inimicus fidei generis

*p n..ch.. edmcer eledos ex orationib; uel historiis alio*
*†? g...? d... inch.... locis*

Saec. X²

Italia settentrionale

...ena tremit · cui patent abissi · quem in...
...rius pauescit · quem omnis irarum motus f...
...cienr humiliatur · te supplex depcor
...minator dñe · ut inuocatione nominis
...tui abhuius famuli tui uexatione inimi
...cus confusus abscedat · & abhuius possessione
anima liberata · ad auctore sue salutis re
curtat · liberatoremq; suu diabolico foe
tore depulso · & odore suauissimo spm
percepto sequat̄ · P ITEM ALIA PRO PAR
uolo ENERGUMINO ▨▨▨▨▨▨▨

Dñe sc̄e pat omps semptne dr̄ · uirtute tua
totis exoro gemitibus · phuius famuli tui
diabolo oppressa infantia · qui etiam indi
gnis interpresuras donas psidium exurge
phuius infantia debellata · & noli diu re
tinere uindictam · nec ante conspectu tui
ueniant parentum delicta · quinec; pfilio
patre · nec pro patre pmisisti filiu iudicari ·
auxiliare qm inimici pauore uexato · ne sine
baptismate facias eius animam a diabolo

such palimpsests are of great interest to the historian, because they often furnish rare old texts. [1] Others of the discarded books were broken up and the folios used either as flyleaves of new volumes or placed into the bindings as reinforcements.[2] Such folios of old volumes occasionally appear when a book is being rebound. These *disiecta membra* of the old manuscripts sometimes provide texts that have all but disappeared.

One such vellum fragment, taken from a binding, now in the Yale manuscript collection (MS 484, no. 6), the gift of Thomas E. Marston, is of unusual interest because it came from a tenth-century copy of a *Sacramentarium Gregorianum*. The fragment consists of a single sheet of vellum, 340 x 275 mm., but on all sides the edges had been turned under approximately 17 mm., indicating that the size of the book into which it had been bound was 235 x 220 mm. Five pairs of double parallel slits show where it was fastened into the original binding. On one side the writing is almost obliterated in places since the whole surface was badly scratched. The writing on the other side which was protected is quite black and entirely legible. The single sheet was originally a bifolium taken from the center fold of a quire of a smaller book, so that it represents four pages. The text, written in a single column with twenty-one lines to a page, occupies approximately 200 x 118 mm. of each page. The script is Caroline minuscule; the headings and the capitals are in red. It would appear to have been copied in France about 900. A few interlinear and marginal notations in a cursive hand are later additions.[3] Fortunately the text is consecutive; beginning with what one may call folio 1$^r$, which is badly rubbed, it continues to 1$^v$ and 2$^r$, which are perfectly clear, then to 2$^v$ which is damaged like 1$^r$.

The text on the fragment consists of seven prayers. The first three, which occur on 1$^r$, are blessings to be invoked at special occasions. The first, *a,* is a short prayer to be offered after a meal. The second, *b,* is a blessing to be invoked upon the new harvest of grapes and beans. The third, *c,* is a blessing to be asked on all of God's gifts. The first two lines of the fourth prayer, *d,* complete the contents of the first page as it continues to the middle of the second page. With the two succeeding prayers, it belongs to a group of *Orationes super energumenos*, that is, petitions for persons who are under the influence of the spirit of evil. The first of these, *d*, is to be made at the imposition of hands upon a catechumen, a candidate for baptism. Another prayer, *e*, this time to ward off the influence of evil from an unbaptized infant, fills the rest of the page and five lines of the third page. A third prayer of exorcism, *f*, fills the page and half of the fourth. It is for a baptized person who has fallen under the power of Satan. The rest of the page is filled with the first half of another prayer of exorcism, *g*, which is broken off at the end of the page.

All of these prayers are found in the *Sacramentarium Gregorianum*. The sacramentary was the chief liturgical book used for services in the Western Church from the fourth to the thirteenth century, when it was superseded entirely by the missal. In addition to the collects for the Mass, it contains various other prayers, blessings, and rites. Great variations occurred, for the book was never standardized. From the many early sacramentaries in use, particularly in Italy and France, there now remain copies of three major ones: the *Leoninum*,[4] used in the seventh century, was associated with the reforms of Pope Leo I and is now preserved in a single manuscript; the *Gelasianum*.[5] named for Pope Gelasius, used particularly in France during the eighth century, is now represented by only one copy; and the *Gregorianum*, also in use in France from the eighth to the tenth century. This last was thought to have been derived from the liturgical reforms of Pope Gregory the Great at the end of the sixth century. Tradition has it that, at the request of Charlemagne, Pope Hadrian I, sometime about 790, sent a copy to the Palace library at Aachen to serve as a model for the liturgy to be followed throughout the realm. To this original sacramentary, Alcuin is said, in 804, to have added a supplementary section with many additional prayers and formulae for various ceremonies. Charlemagne's efforts thus to regularize the liturgy were not entirely successful however, since in many places the old

*Gelasianum* continued in use and other variants named for particular locations were not displaced. After the adoption of the missal, very few copies of the *Sacramentarium Gregorianum* were preserved and not one can be called "official," but a text compiled from three ninth-century manuscripts, two now in the Vatican and one in Cambrai, can certainly be considered representative. It is with this edition[6] that the text of the Yale fragment must be compared.

In the *Sacramentarium Gregorianum* prayer *a* of the fragment is found in a section headed *Orationes super mensas.*[7] It is the very simplest form of grace after meals, to give thanks for the nourishment received and to ask for the blessing of God's mercy. It must have been so commonly used that in the fragment the scribe took the liberty of omitting the final words of the usual formula—"vivis et regnas deus per omnia saecula saeculorum." Prayer *b* comes under the general heading *Benedictiones variae,* with the special caption *Benedictio uvae vel fabae.*[8] This is a graceful prayer of benediction on the new harvest of grapes and beans, the two crops that were the staples of the French and Italian country diet. It was no peasant, however, who composed the felicitous wording: "quod tu domine per rorem caeli et innundantiam pluviarum et tempore serena atque tranquilla ad maturitatem perducere dignatus es." Here, too, although the text is identical with that of the *Gregorianum,* the scribe again omitted the formulaic ending: "nostri Iesu Christi qui tecum vivit." Prayer *c* is a general blessing upon all of God's gifts with the petition that they may be beneficial for the healing of the human race and that whoever partakes of them may live in health of body and wholeness of mind. The dignified wording and the general inclusiveness of the supplication would seem to indicate that this was reserved for special public occasions. It matches the prayer in the *Gregorianum* exactly.[9]

The last four prayers in the fragment come under the heading *Orationes super energumenos* in the *Sacramentarium Gregorianum.*[10] An individual who is *energumenus* (ἐνεργούμενος) is one who is so obsessed with evil thoughts, desires, and actions, that he is judged to be under the influence of or in the possession of the devil. The term, however, was sufficiently comprehensive to cover persons suffering from an alarming physical disease like epilepsy or from a nervous disorder or actual insanity. Furthermore, the word also designated persons who had not yet been baptized and who, therefore, were still under the dominance of original sin, or of Satan. It is necessary, then, to differentiate among the prayers under the general category *Super energumenos* those that were intended to precede and accompany the sacrament of baptism to ward off evil from the new Christian, and those that are specifically prayers of exorcism for demoniacs.

The first two prayers in the fragment are associated with baptism. The first, *d*, is intended for a catechumen who presents himself to be baptized. The candidate, who has gone through a long and disciplined preparation for the rite which should make him a new man, cleansed of sin, comes before the priest for the imposition of hands. Making a solemn prayer to God who controls the heights and depths of the great universe as well as the passions of men, the priest asks that, at the invocation of the divine name, the "enemy." brought to confusion, may cease from persecuting this servant of God, and that his soul, freed from the hold of the evil one, may be restored to the author of its salvation, that he may ever after follow his Saviour now that he has known the sweet fragrance of the Holy Spirit.

The second prayer of exorcism, *e*, is for an unbaptized infant to free him from the power of the evil one. Since at this time the sacrament of baptism was normally reserved for adults who were able to undergo a long initiation, possibly this rite was administered only under unusual circumstances. In this prayer, God, the eternal, the omnipotent, is besought to come to the defence of a child who is beset by the devil. He is implored not to visit the sins of the parents upon the infant but to free his young soul from the vexations of the evil one so that he may live to give thanks ever after.

Both of these prayers are identical with the ones in the *Gregorianum*.[11] Since exorcism was included in the baptismal rite from the time of the third century, it is not surprising that the two prayers are also found in the earlier *Gelasianum*[12] where they are given in a special section on the sacrament of baptism to be administered on the vigil of Pentecost. Although they are not in the modern *Rituale Romanum,* exorcism continues to be a very important feature of the contemporary rite which is normally administered to infants. First of all, in the hallowing of the font, the priest exorcises the water before he blesses it, as he also does with the salt and the holy oil. Both before and after he signs the child with the Cross, he pronounces an exorcism—"Exorcizo te, immunde spiritus"—commanding Satan to depart from the child. Finally, he asks the sponsors to affirm, in the name of the child, that he will renounce the devil and all his works.

The last two prayers in the fragment, *f* and *g,* are for an adult who has been baptized but is now a demoniac. The first is an awesome prayer in which the exorcist first invokes the help of God in all of his aspects as God of angels, arch-angels, prophets, apostles, and martyrs, to grant his priest power over the spirit of evil that he may depart at the sound of the divine name. Then, addressing Satan, he tells him that the God who controls the winds, the seas, and the heights of heaven and the depths of hell commands him to depart. Calling the spirit of evil the most wicked Satan, enemy of the faith, bringer of death to the human race, destroyer of justice, root of all evil, nurse of vices, seducer of men, downfall of nations, inciter to envy, font of avarice, cause of discord, bringer of woes, teacher of demons, the priest commands him to depart conquered by the ever-triumphant God, and to give place to the Holy Spirit. This is precisely the same prayer as that in the *Gregorianum.*[13]

The last prayer, *g,* is a splendid and beautiful supplication to God, the creator and defender of the race of men, who has formed man in his own image, to look down with mercy upon his servant who has fallen a victim to the craftiness of the evil one, and to deliver him from the terrors and consternation into which his mind has been thrown by the wiles of the ancient enemy of the whole world. Unfortunately the prayer is broken off at the end of the last page of the fragment, but it is the same prayer that is found in the *Gregorianum*.[14] Apparently it has been continuously in use since that time, for it is one of the foremost prayers in the modern *Rituale Romanum* under the rite of exorcism.[15]

If some questions raised by the manuscript fragment have been answered, more remain. Where was it written, and precisely when? At what point was the book of which it was a part discarded, and where are the other folios? Where is and what was the book into whose cover it was bound?

*Part II*

Medieval Texts

# A Medieval Textbook

Sometime before 1280, Eberhard the German, who as a student had starved in Paris and in Orleans and then became master of a school in Bremen, wrote a long elegiac poem on the composition and style of poetry which he called *Laborintus*.[1] By the title Eberhard meant not "labyrinth" but "misery," as one discovers from the long introduction and conclusion in which he gives a detailed exposition of the wretchedness of the life of a teacher. Yet, in spite of his bitter awareness of the miseries related to the profession, he apparently taught with enthusiasm, if one may judge by his lively digression on the thirty-seven works of literature that a well-educated young student should read. Beginning with the elementary pupils and always assuming their grounding in Latin from the famous Grammar of Donatus, Eberhard names in order the books suitable for study because of their relative simplicity as well as their value for moral training. These are the *Disticha*, or proverbial sayings attributed to Cato, "the wise, the guide to virtue, the moulder of manners"; the *Ecloga* of Theodulus wherein the author "defends the cause of

truth in a dispute with falsehood"; the *Fabulae* of Avianus,
who "instructs by his fables and draws one from vices"; the
stories of Aesop which "produce flowers that, in turn, yield
fruit, for he is sagacious"; and the *Elegiae* of Maximianus
that realistically describe "the tribulations of old age." For
the boys who have passed from these elementary texts, the
works Eberhard recommends range from Horace, Virgil,
and Juvenal, to Statius and Claudian, through the post-
Classical writers to the *Aurora* of Peter Riga and the *Doctrinale* of Alexandre de Villedieu.

Other educators of the twelfth and thirteenth centuries,
notably Conrad of Hirsau and Alexander Neckham, give lists
of "curriculum authors" similar to Eberhard's,[2] and while
these vary somewhat in the selection of the advanced texts,
they are generally in agreement on the primary books. That
the young boys were all nurtured on the same literary diet is
evidenced by the fact that the introductory texts were frequently
copied together into a single volume.

One of these textbooks written in England about 1300 has
recently come to Yale from the legacy of Edwin J. Beinecke.
It is a small volume (MS 513) of thirty-one vellum leaves,
worn from hard usage and darkened from much thumbing,
particularly the earlier folios. It had long ago lost its original
binding and some of the pages were torn, so that it has had
to be repaired and rebound. It is written in black ink, now
somewhat faded, with red capitals and headings in red, and
contains the *Ecloga* of Theodulus, the *Fabulae* of Avianus,
and the *Elegiae* of Maximianus. The omission of the *Disticha
Catonis*, normally found at the beginning, may indicate that
it had been bound separately, as a kind of first reader. The
absence of Aesop, probably in the Latin version of Phaedrus,
is not surprising, in view of the inclusion of the Fables of
Avianus.

It is rather interesting that the three works in the little textbook are all in poetry. The first, an eclogue in leonine hexameter verse, was written in the tenth century by an author
known only as Theodulus.[3] In the tradition of bucolic poetry,
it is cast in the form of an *altercatio*, a poetic contest between

Pseustis, a goatherd, the personification of falsehood, and Alithia, a shepherdess representing truth, while Fronesis or prudence serves as arbiter. The subject of the debate is pagan myth versus Biblical truth, and the purpose is to demonstrate the victory of Christian doctrine over the old superstitions. Pseustis begins with praise for the story of Saturn and the Golden Age, which Alithia counters with the true version of the perfect state of man, the Garden of Eden; Pseustis describes Deucalion and Pyrrha and the Flood, after which Alithia recounts the revealed history of Noah. Each contestant presents his case in the short space of four verses, and there are thirty-eight topics debated.

The poem would seem to present several difficulties for a young pupil. In the first place the vocabulary is unusual and extensive, the style is too compressed for easy comprehension, and often the meter forces the author into circumlocutions that must have been puzzling. Then the subject matter of all but the most common myths must have been foreign to the experience of the boys, and even some of the less frequently quoted Bible stories must have been unfamiliar. In spite of all these apparent disadvantages, the *Ecloga* was extremely popular, as one may judge from the fact that there remain one hundred and twenty-one manuscripts and it was printed in fifty-four early editions. Normally the text of the *Ecloga* was supplied with a commentary. For example, Bernard of Utrecht[4] in the eleventh century wrote a commentary for it and the early printed texts have commentaries by later writers.[5] In the Yale manuscript a commentary by an unidentified writer fills the spaces between the lines and all the margins with fine writing so that what was originally an uncluttered and attractive page is now crowded and confusing. One suspects that the commentary was of greater use to the master than to the boys, and that, indeed, the teacher really needed it!

After toiling over Theodulus' mythology, surely any boy must have been relieved to advance to the second text of his schoolbook, the *Fabulae* of Avianus. The author, writing about A.D. 400, says that he took these forty-two fables of the

Aesopean corpus chiefly from the version of Babrius, the Greek fabulist of the Augustan Age.[6] They include, besides the usual animal tales, such favorites as the North Wind and the Sun and the Boy and the Thief. Here the young reader would be on familiar ground, since presumably he would have seen ants, grasshoppers, dogs, geese, and sheep, and even though he had no experience with lions, tigers, and monkeys, at least he would have heard of them. The language too is geared to the level of the boys and the style is uncomplicated. The elegiac couplets run along smoothly with an ease somewhat reminiscent of Ovid. There is no Christian orientation to the stories but they seem, in general, to have a kind of peasant version of behaviour for survival in a competitive world. Although originally the fables were not supplied with "morals," in the Yale manuscript, as in most of the schoolbook copies, an epilogue (occasionally a proem) written in medieval times has been added to point out the lesson of the story and to relate it to the reader.

The third text, the *Elegiae* of Maximianus,[7] is hard to justify as suitable reading for a young pupil. Written in the sixth century by a man who called himself an Etruscan and claimed to be a relative of Boethius, the five elegies present a dismal picture of an unlovely old age bereft of all the delights of youth. Whether the author was inventing an elaborate poetic conceit after the manner of the Roman elegiac poets, or was expressing his own disenchantment with life without love and spring and gaiety, the poems provide a depressing portrait of an old man pitiful not because of his lost loves and failing strength, but because, like the grasshopper in the fable, he refuses to accept the fact that winter implacably follows upon summer. If the poems were a cruel warning of *Memento mori*, this seems highly inappropriate for a school reader. Two distinct opinions concerning the matter were voiced by educators of the thirteenth century. Hughes de Trimberg, writing about 1280, praised the "many notable verses" and worthy sentiments;[8] an unnamed author of *Accessus ad auctores* says that the purpose was to expose stupid wishes and warn against the foolish desires of old age.[9] On the other hand, Alexandre de Villedieu called the elegies *nugae,* trifling verses, which should be removed from the curriculum.[10]

Nowhere is there any record of the schoolboys' reaction— submission, resistance, or withdrawal—to this more or less standardized textbook. Yet one can, quite indirectly, find some indication of the situation written between the lines of another textbook, that of Egbert of Liège, the *Fecunda ratis,* which was written about 1020.[11] Egbert apparently enjoyed teaching, knew how to teach, and, more important, he liked his pupils, particularly the small boys whom he called his "little mice." So he tried to devise a schoolbook that they would find an attractive introduction to learning. His book, the "Well-laden Ship," very suitably titled for boys living along the Meuse, is filled with good things, even if the poetry is not uniformly superior. For the young children "still frightened by the new experience of discipline," the prow holds a variety of memorable sayings taken largely from the Classical writers, at first arranged in one or two lines, then in three or four. Some of these proverbs were given pertinence by being located in familiar settings. So, for example, "Rome was not built in a day" becomes "The lofty palace at Aachen was not built in a single year." The second part of the book, the stern of the ship, is filled with a great variety of longer passages adapted from the Bible, the Fathers, fables, epigrams, etc. In addition to the Classical and Biblical references there are some allusions to the contemporary scene, even a few humorous selections and one the prototype of Little Red Riding Hood. In the midst of these passages there is one rather long poem devoted to the cruel and lazy teachers who stupidly demand of their pupils what they never taught them. For some unexplained reason this unique little book was never used very widely. It is preserved in a single manuscript (Cologne 196) of the eleventh century. Placed beside the traditional textbook, it would seem to say loudly that a schoolbook should be attractive, that it should contain relevant and interesting material, and that the teacher should be intelligent and sympathetic.

# Johannes Climacus'
## Ladder of Divine Ascent

"What is this mystery in me? What is the meaning of this blending of body and soul? How am I constituted a friend and foe to myself? Tell me, my yoke fellow, my nature, for I shall not ask anyone else in order to learn about you."[1] These words come not from a modern student agonizing over the problem of identity, trying to make peace with himself, but from a Greek monk, abbot of a monastery on Mount Sinai, about A.D. 600. They occur in a treatise on the cultivation of the spiritual life which the writer called Κλῖμαξ θείας ἀνόδου, but which is more commonly known as the *Scala Paradisi*, or the *Ladder of Divine Ascent*.[2]

The author is known only as Johannes, sometimes with the epithet Scholasticus, but he is usually designated as Climacus from the title of his book. His whole life was spent on the Sinai peninsula where he lived for forty years as a solitary monk before he became abbot of the monastery there. In spite of his limited experience with the world, he seems to have read widely, and certainly he acquired deep insight into human nature. His book, the title of which was inspired by Jacob's

vision of the ladder to Heaven (*Genesis* 28.12), was designed
for the monks as a guide to attaining perfection in their spiritual lives. It is divided into thirty chapters or rungs on the
ladder, one for each of the thirty unchronicled years in the life
of Christ. The first three chapters deal with the conditions of
mind and spirit necessary for anyone who is considering
entering upon the religious life. The succeeding steps are
concerned with the virtues that must be cherished and nour-
ished and the vices that must be extirpated from one's nature.
The man who successfully climbs to this point achieves tran-
quillity, the twenty-ninth rung. He has then only to advance to
the last, faith, hope, and charity, which constitute spiritual
perfection.

As the symbolism of the ladder of divine ascent that
Johannes Climacus used to make vivid his idea of the way of
spiritual progress toward perfection was certainly not original
with him, so also the same imagery was used frequently by
later writers who had no knowledge of his work. One may cite,
for example, the allegory of the *Scala Paradisi* attributed to St.
Bernard in the twelfth century and Walter Hilton's *Scale of
Perfection* in the fourteenth century. No more original or
exclusive was Climacus' assumption that solitude for contemplation is a most necessary requisite for the attainment
of his goal. From St. Paul's injunction to the Thessalonians
(IV.II): "Study to be quiet," to George Herbert and the
English metaphysical poets, to Thoreau the hermit of Walden
Pond, down to the *Seeds of Contemplation* of Thomas Merton,
the practice of silent meditation as the means to gaining a
glimpse of the divine mysteries has been advocated. Perhaps
more unexpected and so more remarkable than Climacus'
use of the ladder metaphor and his stress upon "holy quiet"
is his emphasis upon the absolute necessity for honest and
complete self-examination. The Greek admonition, "Know
thyself," which Socrates spent his life supporting, was not,
as a general rule, an approach sanctioned by heads of
authoritarian communities. Yet Climacus, who somehow
acquired a penetrating insight into the workings of men's
minds and emotions, is alert to all the machinations by

which men delude themselves. So by means of numerous examples from secular life he exposes common situations wherein a man attempts to deceive others but actually defrauds himself. Often by using metaphors and similes from everyday life, he uncovers the more subtle ways in which even the seemingly completely devout and dedicated religious sometimes negates his own efforts because of improper motives of which he may not even be aware. Like a psychiatrist, Climacus tries to induce the individual to probe the deep channels of his own mind and to analyze his own spiritual condition. The thirty steps can be mounted only by men who have gained control over their own natures sufficiently to profit by the guidance of their instructor.

Johannes Climacus' *Ladder* quickly gained a very much wider circle of readers than the monks on Mount Sinai, and it continued to be read throughout those parts of the East that were under the control of the Orthodox Church. There are extant a large number of Greek manuscripts of the work preserved chiefly in the libraries of Greece and the eastern European countries. Some of these later ones apparently were showpieces, for they are profusely illustrated with elaborate drawings of the ladder, showing some people ascending, some falling back, and a very few struggling to the top.[3]

In the Beinecke Library a manuscript hitherto designated as a treatise on the virtues and vices has recently been discovered to contain the text of the *Ladder of Divine Ascent*. This manuscript (MS 237) is a small thick volume of 219 vellum leaves, bound in old brown leather. It was written sometime in the thirteenth century, in a clear hand in black ink with initials and headings in red. The text is complete. On the last two folios, in red, there are drawings of three separate ladders with an explanation of the meaning of each rung, but there are no human figures. Clearly this book was intended for study rather than exhibition, and it must have been long used and constantly studied, for the parchment is yellow and discolored and the fore-corners of the leaves are rounded and worn from much turning.

The early history of this manuscript is unknown, except that it was copied somewhere in the Byzantine East, undoubtedly by a monk. Early in the last century it came into the possession of the English dealer, Thomas Thorpe, who sold it to Sir Thomas Phillipps, the famous book collector (MS 4289). After one of the auction sales of his great library, it was brought to New Haven by Laurence C. Witten. In 1957 it was presented to Yale with other Greek manuscripts as a gift of the Jacob Ziskind Trust.[4]

Climacus' Greek treatise was early translated into Syriac, Arabic, Armenian, and Church Slavonic, then into Russian, Serbian, and Bulgarian. The western world first became aware of the *Ladder* through a Latin translation made by Angelus de Cingulo in 1294, but there is little evidence of its influence in Europe. A hundred years later, a more important Latin translation with interpretations by the translator was made by the Italian humanist and monk of the Camaldolite Order, Ambrogio Traversari. A late edition of this version, published in Cologne in 1583, is in the Beinecke Library. Like the other works of this learned scholar, Ambrogio's translation had a large circle of readers, and a number of translations into the vernaculars were made from his Latin text. An Italian translation was published in Venice in 1491, and seven Spanish translations appeared in the sixteenth century. One of these, *Escalera espiritual de San Juan Climaco*, translated by Fray Juan de Estrada, is of special interest, for, published in Mexico in 1535, it was one of the very first books to be printed in America.[5]

3. Portrait of Walter Burley with four philosophers

Beinecke Rare Book and Manuscript Library, Yale University Marston MS 91, f.1r.

# WALTER BURLEY'S

## *De Vita et Moribus Philosophorum*

No one would dispute the truth of the aphorism attributed to Donatus that it would be far less difficult to wrest his club from Hercules than to steal a single verse from Homer. For writers of smaller stature, however, the case would have been quite different, particularly in the Middle Ages. Then it must have been easy and relatively safe to pirate even an entire book. Yet, strangely enough, this kind of plagiarism was rare. It seems all the more remarkable then that, long after the Middle Ages, in 1603, an Italian lawyer, Anastasius a Sala, did have printed and attempted to pass off as his own a very famous book indeed.[1]

The rash purloiner must have been inordinately impressed by the work to take the risk involved in appropriating it. Written more than two and a half centuries earlier by the English scholar, Walter Burley, it had hosts of other admirers. If one uses the simple criterion of popularity, this by-product of Burley's serious work in philosophy far outshadowed and outlived all of his erudite treatises on Aristotle. Long before the end of the sixteenth century, this book, the *De vita et mori-*

*bus philosophorum* (The Lives and Manners of the Philosophers), had been circulated all over Europe, for over 150
manuscripts of it are still extant. It had been printed in thirty
editions by 1530. For a wider audience it was translated into
Spanish in the early fifteenth century, into Italian by 1475, into
German (by two different translators) by 1490, and into Polish
in three versions by the beginning of the sixteenth century.[2]

Burley, often designated *doctor planus et perspicuus* for
his precise and lucid writings, was born in 1275, probably in
Yorkshire, and was educated at Merton College, Oxford.[3]
His early interest in philosophy led him to Paris where he
became a pupil of Duns Scotus and a fellow-student with
William of Ockham and where, in a later sojourn, he received
the degree of Doctor of Theology. Although he has always
been associated with the Franciscans, he was probably a secular priest. Twice, in 1327 and 1330, he went on diplomatic
missions to the Papal Court at Avignon. His teaching posts
extended from Oxford and the Sorbonne to Toulouse and
Bologna. In his later years he served as tutor to Edward Prince
of Wales (1330-76), popularly known as the Black Prince. As a
member of the official household of Richard de Bury, Bishop
of Durham, Burley held a number of ecclesiastical benefices
in England until his death about 1345. Throughout his life he
was occupied chiefly with the study of philosophy, however,
and enjoyed great prestige both in England and on the Continent for his achievements in that field. He is credited with
130 treatises on Aristotle and a large number of commentaries
on later exponents of Aristotelianism. Many of these texts
became standard books in the schools. Curiously, his philosophical position has been variously interpreted; Sarton[4]
indicates the diversity of opinion when he says, "He was
more of a realist than a nominalist."

Burley would seem to have written the *De vita et moribus
philosophorum* rather late in his career, probably while he
was in southern Europe, for almost all of the manuscripts
derive from Italy and France, with later ones from Germany
and Bohemia. Although there are many variations, including
abridgments, the text usually contains accounts of 132 Greek

and Roman philosophers, poets, historians, and statesmen, from Thales to the sixth-century Latin grammarian Priscian. The Beinecke Library owns two manuscripts of the Latin original. The first (Marston MS 80) is included in a group of moralistic texts of Italian origin, copied about 1410. In this version, which would appear to have been used as a school-book, the work has been severely abbreviated. The second manuscript (Marston MS 91) is a handsome volume copied in the fifteenth century. It is of particular interest for on the first page there is an illuminated initial with a charming portrait in lively colors of Burley himself, standing before a lectern with an open book. On the same page there are four smaller portraits of philosophers. Although this version contains only seventy-six biographies, the text is good and is carefully written. The Beinecke Library owns also the three earliest incunabular editions of the work: two (Cologne, 1470, and Nuremberg, 1477) of the Latin text, and the third, (Augsburg, 1490,) of a German translation.

Besides all these, two more texts of the *De vita* have recently been unmasked in the Library where they had been hiding under the name of Diogenes Laertius, the Greek biographer of the early third century.[5] Both are of an Italian translation, the first a fifteenth-century manuscript (Marston MS 114), the other an early edition printed in Venice in 1535. On the manuscript there is no title or author's name, and the text begins at once with the life of Thales. The printed edition, on the other hand, has this title (as translated): "Lives of the Moral Philosophers and Their Memorable Sayings Taken from Laertius and Other Ancient Authors." The Italian translator was misled by numerous references, such as "As Laertius says," "As Seneca says," and "As Cicero says," into assuming that this was indeed essentially a compilation of material drawn directly from the original sources. On the contrary, the quo-tations are largely taken at secondhand, and the work is thoroughly medieval. I should like to demonstrate this by considering briefly the contents, the general treatment of the material, the sources, and the tone of Burley's book.

Burley's compilation does, to be sure, contain the lives of

the ancient Greek philosophers that Diogenes Laertius had treated, but it has also the lives of later writers such as Plutarch, Plotinus, and Porphyrios (third century A.D.), as well as the Roman philosophers Seneca and Chalcidius (fourth century A. D.). There are also lives of poets, for example, Homer, Simonides, Aeschylus, Sophocles, and Euripides, along with the Romans Plautus, Terence, Horace, Ovid, Virgil, and even Claudianus (fourth century A.D.). Orators and statesmen range from Pericles, Demosthenes, Themistocles, and Ptolemy Philadelphus among the Greeks, to Cato, Scipio, and Cicero among the Romans. Science is represented by Hippocrates, Archimedes, Galen, Pliny the Elder, and Claudius Ptolemy. In a miscellaneous group there are Aesop, Valerius Maximus, Aurelius Symmachus, and Priscian the sixth-century grammarian. The most unexpected biographies are those of the magician, Hermes Trismegistos, and Zoroaster.

The lives vary in length from two lines to five or six pages according to the material available. So far as was possible, dates were given. With the Greek writers of the pre-Christian era, the date is usually indicated by reference to the Hebrew kings or prophets. The Romans are located in time with relation to some other prominent Roman. Anecdotes are given to illustrate the character of the person. In numerous instances, the device is employed of reporting a series of questions put to the great man, with his succinct and wise answers. Usually the literary works of the subjects are identified.

The sources upon which Burley drew for his biographies are largely medieval. (If he used Diogenes Laertius for the Greek philosophers, he must have read a twelfth-century Latin translation, for he did not know Greek.) Besides Cicero and Seneca, he cites Aulus Gellius, Valerius Maximus, Solinus, Jerome, Augustine, Boethius, and Isidore of Seville. Yet many of these citations, as well as the quotations from Diogenes Laertius, can be traced to the great encyclopedia, the *Speculum maius* of the French Dominican friar, Vincent of Beauvais. This vast compendium of all knowledge was used by Burley as his chief source. Another rich field of information from which he drew, particularly for aphorisms and precepts, was the *Compendiloquium*, a work of the thirteenth-century English Franciscan, John of Wales. Nowhere does Burley give credit to these two sources, but he does name two twelfth-century scholars, Alexander Neckham and Bernard Silvester, for specific references.

Finally, one should note what might be called the medieval flavor of the biographies. Burley was giving what he knew would appeal to his readers. Consequently, when he writes of Epimenides of Crete (the prototype of Rip van Winkle), he repeats the story of his fifty-seven year sleep and bewilderment upon returning to an unfamiliar world, but brings the biography to a climax with an account of how Epimenides delivered Athens from the plague by setting up an altar to the unknown god, an incident that good Christians would immediately associate with Paul's remarks in his sermon on the Areopagus. In the life of Homer (who lived at the time of King Saul), Burley does credit the poet with the creation of the Iliad and the Odyssey, but devotes most of his space to a silly tale of how the poet (who lived to be 108) took his own life in desperation at being unable to solve a riddle posed by some crude fisherman! He treats Zoroaster briefly as a magician who, unlike the totality of mankind who come into the world weeping, was born laughing, an indication of an unnatural defiance of this vale of tears. His account of Virgil is given over completely to the medieval legends of his powers as a wonder-worker; that he made, among other marvels, a bronze fly which, when placed at the city gate of Naples, drove all the other flies from the city; that he constructed an ingenious bridge of air by which he transported himself wherever he wished to go; and that, in Rome, he built a palace containing wooden statues representing the various provinces, each holding a bell that rang whenever there was trouble in that particular province.

Since Burley's purpose in the *De vita* was didactic and his approach moralistic, an important part of each biography lists the man's notable sayings. These may be precepts, definitions, maxims, or memorable dicta, and are for the most part noncontroversial statements of universal application and general admonitions suitable for all civilized persons. If doctrines antipathetic to Christian teachings are included, they are accompanied by words of warning. Thus, after praising several maxims of Epicurus, Burley adds:

> Nevertheless he was in error on more points than most philosophers, for he thought that God has no concern for human affairs, and he said that pleasure is the highest good and that men's souls perish with their bodies.

As one might expect, the memorable sayings deal chiefly with such topics as the nature of man, the soul, the cardinal virtues, and wisdom. They are for the most part the familiar aphorisms that one finds repeated later in collections of quotations on moral philosophy. Yet Burley gives an unusually high proportion of sayings on the subject of friendship, mentioning the essays of Theophrastus and of Cicero, and giving many of their thoughts on the value of friendship, as, for instance, the dictum of Theophrastus that "A man without a friend is like a body without a soul."

Burley wrote his book in the third person, and, since he injected no personal references, it is difficult to discover what manner of man he was. In view of the fact that he studied in at least two great universities, taught in various cities, traveled extensively, and had experience in a number of ecclesiastical posts, he must have developed a certain cosmopolitan point of view. One is tempted to apply to him an anecdote that he tells of the philosopher Aristippus, who, when asked what he had gained from philosophy, answered, "The ability to communicate with all men."[6]

# THE APOCRYPHAL ABGARUS-JESUS EPISTLES
# IN ENGLAND IN THE MIDDLE AGES

In the East the legend of the healing of King Abgarus and
the conversion of the kingdom of Edessa to Christianity was
widely known and fervently cherished from the time of its
origin. Apparently it started with two Syriac letters, one said
to be written to Jesus by Abgarus Uchomo,[1] ruler of the Meso-
potamian kingdom of Edessa, and the other said to be the
answer of Jesus. In his letter Abgarus, suffering from a deadly
disease assumed to be leprosy, begged Jesus to come to Edessa
to heal him and there to find asylum from the persecution he
was experiencing in Jerusalem. The gracious answer, delivered
by the messenger, Ananias, explained that, since the end was
very near, Jesus would not be able to go to Edessa, but he
promised that later one of his disciples would go to cure the
king of his illness.[2]

From this nucleus the legend grew to include an account
of the miraculous powers of Jesus' letter which was copied
and used as an amulet for individuals, while the original was
a palladium for Edessa. Another later addition is the story
that the messenger also procured a portrait of Jesus miracu-

lously imprinted upon a linen cloth. The Syriac *Doctrina Addai* or *Acts of Thaddeus* soon rounded out the legend with the account of the healing of Abgarus and others by Thaddeus (also called Judas or Jude), who was sent by St. Thomas the Apostle, and the subsequent conversion of Abgarus and of Edessa.[3] There is even a sequel from the martyrdom of St. Thomas which states that about two hundred years after his death, the body of the saint was sent by the Emperor Alexander to Edessa for entombment.[4]

The West had its first knowledge of the legend in the *Peregrinatio Aetheriae ad loca sacra,* the remarkable account of the long pilgrimage made about 380 by the Spanish nun, Aetheria, to the East to visit all the sites of the Holy Land. She describes the historical monuments in Edessa that were associated with King Abgarus and says that she prayed at the tomb of St. Thomas. What impressed her most, however, was seeing the actual letters, written in Syriac on vellum, of the King and Jesus, which were considered the greatest treasure of the city.[5] The Bishop of Edessa graciously gave her copies of the letters as mementoes of her visit and as a powerful talisman for her protection, though strangely enough she remarks that she had a copy of them back in her homeland.[6] The fact that this remarkable account of an unusual journey made by a woman in the fourth century has been preserved in only one manuscript, an eleventh-century copy originating at Monte Cassino,[7] may explain why it was not known more generally in the Middle Ages.

It was not the *Peregrinatio* of Aetheria, however,[8] but rather the Latin translation made by Rufinus about 402 of the Greek *Ecclesiastical History* of Eusebius that disseminated the legend throughout Europe.[9] In the thirteenth chapter of the first book of his great history, written about 311, Eusebius says that in Edessa he saw the famous letters of Abgarus and Jesus in the state archives[10] and that he translated them from Syriac into Greek. Not only does he give the translation, but he presents a full account of the circumstances of their composition, followed by the complete narrative supplied by the *Acts of Thaddeus*.[11]

¶ Epta Abgari ad Ihm

Abgar<sup></sup> Euchamae fili9 toparcha · Ihm saluatori bono q̄ apparuit in loco hierosolimoꝝ Salutē. Auditū m̄ est et d̄ te, et d̄ sanitatib9 quas facis, ꝙ sine medicament aut herbis facis ista per te. Et q̄ Verbo tantū cecos facis videre, claudos ambulare, et lepꝛos mundas et immūdos spūs ac demones eicis. Et eos q̄ longo egritudineb9 affligūt · curas et sanas. mortuos q̄ suscitas. Quib9 oīb9 auditis d̄ te · statuī aio meo vnū ex de duob9, aut ꝙ tu sis deus. Et de scendens de celo vt h̄ facias, aut q̄ q̄ fili9 dei sis q̄ h̄ facis. Propterea ergo scibens rogaui te vt digneris vsꝗ ad me fatigari. et egritudinē meam, qua iam diu laboro · curare. Nam et audio q̄ Iudei murmurant aduersum te et Volūt t insidiari. Est autē ciuitas mea parua quidem s̄ honesta · que sufficiat vtrisꝗ. ——

—— Ob. in Anglia 92 · ꝯ̄dd̄.
Apr̄ll · 8 · d · Ville ·
Et sep̄ 2g · Apr̄ll · p · 11 · octie pochede.

—— Obꝰ · quintedecie reaꝝ Anglie · 3ꝉ · Aprl 933 · t.
g · d · ob · de claro Vꝉr exped Ġollecto wꝝ.

4. Abgarus' Letter to Jesus

Beinecke Rare Book and Manuscript Library, Yale University Marston MS 252, f.iiir.

Modern scholars believe that the Abgarus-Jesus letters were composed about A.D. 200.[12] The Roman Church did not adjudicate on the subject until 495 when the so-called *Decretum Gelasianum* was promulgated and the authenticity of the letters was rejected.[13] Since then they have been properly designated as the Abgarus-Jesus Epistles of the Apocryphal New Testament.[14] Perhaps, however, the papal decree was not generally known in northern Europe, for the letters continued to be quoted as genuine. The only reference in early medieval times to the problem of their authenticity that I have found occurs in a work attributed to Haimo that can be dated about 825. In the *Enchiridion de Christianarum rerum memoria*, which is a kind of epitome of Eusebius' *History*, Haimo says, when mentioning the mission of Thaddeus to Edessa, "I have found this account discussed at greater length in some writing, but I do not know if it is apocryphal— that God alone knows—but I have decided to include it here because it derives from true faith."[15]

In England, the first witness to the Abgarus letters, which apparently were still accepted as genuine, is found in a manuscript originally from St. Edmund's Abbey that contains an Anglo-Saxon version of both letters copied in the tenth century.[16] Another British Museum manuscript, written in a Benedictine monastery in Northumbria at the end of the tenth century, gives the Latin text of Jesus' letter to Abgarus.[17] About the year 1000, the great scholar and poet, Aelfric, composed his *Lives of the Saints* arranged according to the Church calendar. For July 30, after his account of the martyrs Abdon and Sennes, he adds the story of Abgarus and gives the two letters.[18] Nowhere has the tale been told with greater charm than in this Anglo-Saxon poetry. Although Aelfric was following Eusebius-Rufinus, he was not restricted by a literal translation, and he even gives the Latin of Jesus' letter before he translates it. He also adds the story of the mission of Thaddeus and the conversion of Abgarus and his people.

A hundred years later, Ordericus Vitalis, the Anglo-Norman chronicler (1075-1143), in his great *Ecclesiastical History*, used the Rufinus translation of Eusebius as his source for the Abgarus letters and the mission of Thaddeus, which he gives in some detail, as well as the account of the portrait of Jesus and the entombment of St. Thomas.[19] Early in the thirteenth century, another English author, Gervasius of Tilbury, who became an international scholar and lived for a time at the court of the Emperor Otto IV, made use of the Abgarus letters and the story of the portrait in his *Otia imperialia.*[20]

In the same century, Vincent of Beauvais produced his great encyclopedia, the *Speculum maius,* known and read not only all over Europe but in England as well. In the section entitled *Speculum historiale*[21] he gives the Abgarus legend from Eusebius-Rufinus, including the story of the portrait and the later mission of Thaddeus. He also refers to a letter of Pope Hadrian I to Charlemagne in which reference is made to the miraculous portrait.[22]

Another non-English writer, Jacobus de Voragine (1228-1296), the Italian Dominican who composed the monumental *Legenda aurea* of saints' lives arranged according to the Church calendar, has a greater right to be included in a study of the legend in England. Under October 26, Jacobus gives the lives of St. Simon and St. Jude, and since St. Jude is also known as St. Thaddeus, the author takes the opportunity to recount the story of Abgarus, the letters, and the healing and conversion of the king. He names Eusebius as his source.[23] It was this great book that William Caxton translated and adapted into English as the *Golden Legend,* in 1483, and printed among the first books from his press. Here, for the first time, since Caxton's book was very popular, the legend had the possibility of reaching a large audience in England.[24]

Even as printing was beginning to replace the hand-written book, the Abgarus-Jesus letters were still being copied, as is evidenced by a manuscript version in the Yale Library. Manuscript 252 of the Marston collection is a fine little vellum volume of Gautier de Chatillon's poem *Gesta Alexandri Magni,* copied in England about 1200. Some time later, apparently the first part of the book was mutilated, for the Prologue was lost. Two centuries later it was replaced by a copy in a hand imitating the original, and four more folios were added at the beginning of the volume when the book was rebound. These first four fifteenth-century folios are completely unrelated to the main text, as they are filled with miscellaneous material in several hands and include a number of Latin aphorisms, a few notes in English, among them a remedy for a sick horse, and finally, in Latin, the letter of Abgarus to Jesus. Written in a clear neat hand, it is a faithful copy of the letter as it occurs in Eusebius-Rufinus.[25] It would be of great interest to know who was responsible for copying it and placing it in such motley company. Until this can be determined, one must only draw the conclusion that the Abgarus legend not only survived, but was accepted as genuine and so continued to be copied up until the end of the Middle Ages in England.[26]

# A Fourteenth-Century Argument
## for an International Date Line

When the Yankee traders sailing around the Cape of Good Hope and the English and European merchantmen rounding the Horn in search of cargoes from the East returned home, they encountered the practical problem of a discrepancy in their reckoning of time. With the increase in shipping, the complete confusion resulting from the use by the various nations of differing prime meridians for determining longitude made some kind of uniformity imperative. Eventually, in 1884, an International Congress for the Purpose of Fixing a Prime-Meridian and a Universal Day was held in Washington. There the agreement to recognize as zero meridian a line in the Pacific 180 degrees from Greenwich and a cosmic day of 24 hours with the corresponding division of the surface of the globe into 24 equidistant parts amounted to a general acceptance of an International Date Line.

For the Portuguese navigators three and a half centuries earlier, the phenomenon of the gain of a day on the journey west around the world and the loss of a day on the eastern journey had been a source of great puzzlement. For this we have the testimony of Antonio Pigafetta, the eyewitness chronicler of Magellan's voyage around the globe. In his diary he records:

> On Wednesday, the ninth of July [1522] we arrived at one of these islands named Santiago [Cape Verde], where we immediately sent the boat ashore to obtain provisions. . . . And we charged our men . . . that, when they were ashore, they should ask what day it was. They were answered that to the Portuguese it was Thursday, at which they were much amazed, for to us it was Wednesday, and we knew not how we had fallen into error. For every day I, being always in health, had written down each day without any intermission. But, as we were told since, there had been no mistake, for we had always made our voyage westward and had returned to the same place of departure as the sun, wherefore the long voyage had brought the gain of twenty-four hours, as is clearly seen.[1]

What was a matter of practical concern for the early mariners and merchant seamen presented a theoretical paradox for the fourteenth-century French scientist, Nicolas Oresme (1320?-1382). His unpublished *Tractatus sperae*, translated from his French *Traitié de l'espere*, is preserved in a contemporary manuscript in the Beinecke Rare Book and Manuscript Library (MS 335), the gift of Mrs. W. Redmond Cross.[2] This treatise consists of fifty chapters and is illustrated by fifteen diagrams. In it the author discusses the form and arrangement of the universe, the order and movement of the planets, the four elements, and, in greater detail, the earth. In the preface, which explains that the work is intended not for astronomers but for ordinary educated men, Oresme refers to an artificial sphere, a model of the earth within the celestial sphere, showing the sun, moon, planets, and various heavenly circles as well as the earth's axis, latitude, longitude, zones, and climates.

Of special relevance to the present topic is the thirty-ninth chapter of the treatise where Oresme presents "a remarkable circling of the earth." In the preceding chapter he had theorized that it would be possible for a man to go around the

5. Oresme demonstrating astronomy to a group of students
Paris, Bibliothèque nationale
MS fr. 1350, f.1r.

earth in a straight line, in one zone. Here he asks the reader to assume that a man might make such a journey in twelve days. He explains that going east the traveler will have shorter days than the "natural" one of twenty-four hours, and going west he will have longer ones. Thus heading west the man will have a 26-hour day, will cover 32½ degrees of the earth's surface each day, and will complete the journey in eleven days. If he goes in the opposite direction, he will have a day of 22 and 2/13 hours, will cover 27 and 9/13 degrees a day, and will take thirteen days to cover the entire distance. Oresme introduces two men to perform an experiment: Petrus will make such an imaginary journey around the world going eastward, beginning at the same time and going at the same speed as Johannes who will head westward. He concludes that if both men return at the same time, that is, after twelve natural days, Johannes will say that he spent eleven days and nights, but Petrus will say that he spent thirteen days and nights on the way. A third man, Robertus, remaining at the starting point, will maintain that twelve days have elapsed since the travelers set out. If the day of the return is actually Sunday, Johannes will say that it is Saturday, but Petrus will insist that it is Monday.

Oresme's *Traitié de l'espere* (which was printed twice very early in the sixteenth century) occurs in seven manuscripts, of which the best is in the Bibliothèque nationale (fr. 1350). One noteworthy feature of the Paris manuscript is a drawing on the first leaf representing the master, presumably Oresme himself, demonstrating a model of the earth and the celestrial spheres to a group of young students. Although the French treatise covers the same material as the Latin *Tractatus*, there are some interesting differences in detail. For example, the French version begins: "Le monde est tout ront aussi comme une pelote," while the Latin reads: "Mundum tanquam pomum dicimus esse rotundum." The French comparison of the earth to a ball is less picturesque than the Latin simile of the round apple, which, incidentally, reminds one of Martin Behaim's famous terrestrial globe, known as his "Erdapfel." In the French version, of course, the travelers are named Jehan and Pierre, with Robert as referee.

This question of the apparent disparity in time between the journey eastward and the journey westward had not been touched upon by earlier medieval writers on astronomy, not even by Oresme's immediate predecessor, Sacro Bosco, in his treatise *De sphaera.* Curiously enough, Oresme's successor, the illustrious Pierre d'Ailly (1350-1420), who in his *Ymago mundi* borrowed long sections from Oresme's treatise,[3] made no reference to this chapter and the imaginary journey. Yet the problem had long fascinated Oresme and he treated it in several others of his works. First, early in his career, he had written his *Quaestiones supra speram,* a series of clarifications of questions based upon Sacro Bosco's *De sphaera.* Oresme's treatise is preserved in a single manuscript now in the Wissenschaftliche Bibliothek of Erfurt (Ampl.Q.299. ff. 113-126); it has not been published, but long quotations from it are given in an article by V. P. Zoubov.[4] Oresme is considering the question as to whether the entire area between the Tropic of Cancer and the Arctic Circle is habitable. Affirming that it has the potentials for habitation, he proposes an imaginary experiment. Suppose Plato and Socrates set out from the same place, at the same time, at the same speed, to go around the globe in the same zone, but in opposite directions. Petrus, remaining at the starting point, counts twenty-five days when the philosophers return, Plato from his westward course logging twenty-four days, and Socrates from his eastward course counting twenty-six. If Petrus, the "control," waits twenty-five days, he will have spent 600 hours. Since Plato finishes the journey in twenty-four days, he must cover one twenty-fourth of the circumference in one day, hence his day must equal twenty-five hours. On the other hand, if Socrates witnesses the sunrise twenty-six times, he will accomplish one twenty-sixth of the journey in a single day, and that day will be 23 and 1/13 hours long.

Some twenty years after the *Quaestiones,* in 1377, at the command of Charles V of France, Oresme made a French translation of Aristotle's *De caelo et mundo.* This *Traitié du ciel et du monde*[5] is more a commentary than a simple translation of the Latin version of the original Greek, for Oresme makes it relevant to his country and his time by inserting illustrations of his own. Thus, at the end of Book II, Chapter 31, he refers to the thirty-ninth chapter of his *Traitié de l'espere*, adding that a bird or a man making such a journey around the world, going straight east, would have one day and one night more by the calendar than one who remained on the spot, just as one who went directly west would have a day and a night less than one who remained in place. Consequently, if both made their journeys at the same time, the one who went east would have two calendar days more than the one who went west. Oresme then quotes a twenty-four line Latin poem which he says he had written some time before. It is concerned with a similar hypothetical journey in which Johannes and Petrus are replaced by A and B, while Robertus becomes C, and the actual time is nine days. Here A, going westward, experiences eight days and nights, while B sees the sun rise and set ten times. To make it more vivid, the day of the return is a memorable one, Easter Day. For A, however, it is still the last day of fasting of the somber season of Lent, while B believes that he has passed the joyous celebration of Easter and that it is Monday. The conclusion of the poem expresses the paradox: "Thus eight, nine, and ten are not just about the same, but they are exactly identical."[6]

Since all of these "experiments" are purely imaginary, the actual time, nine, twelve, or twenty-five days, makes no difference. Oresme knew the length of the circumference of the earth as given by Macrobius[7] and generally accepted by medieval scientists, that is, 252,000 Roman stades or 31,500 Roman miles. He also calculated how long it would take to traverse it. In the twenty-sixth chapter of his *Tractatus* he states that if it were possible for a man to walk around the earth at the equator, going twenty Roman miles a day, he would complete the journey in four years, sixteen weeks, and two days. In the *Traitié du ciel et du monde* he says that if a man were walking on a circle closer to the pole, for example at fifty degrees, the latitude of Rouen, the journey would naturally be shorter. At the end of chapter 39 of the *Tractatus*, he points out that for purposes of illustration it would make no difference if one took 100 or 1,000 days, for there would always be two days' variance for the two travelers.

However concerned Oresme was with these questions of the terrestrial globe, his fame does not derive from his work in astronomy and geometry. During his lifetime he was widely recognized for his activities as a teacher and as an ecclesiastical administrator. Originally from a village in Normandy near Caen, he was educated at the College of Navarre at the University of Paris, where presumably he received a doctor's degree, for he became the grand master of his college in 1356. In 1362 he was appointed canon at the cathedral of Rouen, and in the following year was given a semi-prebend at Notre Dame de Paris. In 1364 he became dean of the cathedral of Rouen and, finally, in 1377 was appointed bishop of Lisieux.[8]

During the course of a busy career of teaching and preaching in the university and the Church, as well as advising Charles V at the royal court, Oresme wrote a large number of books on a diversity of subjects which reveal his wide interests and comprehensive knowledge. Of these treatises, some of which are still unpublished, several made a special impact upon his contemporaries. For example, in the field of political economy he wrote first in Latin and then translated into French a work on the origin, nature, law, and fluctuations of money (*De origine, natura, jure et mutationibus monetarum*). This original essay, for which he is best known today, supplemented his French translations of Aristotle's *Politics*, *Ethics*, and *Economics*, which were the first translations of these works into any vernacular language. In the mathematical sciences Oresme wrote a series of important works, from an early *Quaestiones super geometriam Euclidis* to a group of original works *Tractatus proportionum*. In addition to the treatises in the field of astronomy already mentioned, one should note his scholarly work *De commensurabilitate aut incommensurabilitate motuum celestium* and his *De luce stellarum* though perhaps Oresme himself would have placed greater emphasis upon his writings against astrology and superstition, the *Contra astrologos* and *Contra divinatores horoscopios.* Treating the physical sciences, he wrote several notable essays, for example, *"Quaestiones super Phisicam* and *De metheoris.* Theology, metaphysics, mechanics, and architecture complete the list of categories into which his writings fall.

Oresme the polymath has been accorded singular distinction by historians of science because of his significant work in three disciplines. In the field of economics he has been considered a predecessor of Gresham[9] because of his ideas on monetary theory; in astronomy a precursor of Copernicus[10] for his conjectures on the diurnal rotation of the earth; and in mathematics a forerunner of Descartes[11] for his work in analytical geometry. Surely he deserves another citation as a pioneer for his treatment of the problem of the world calendar. In one of the examples he gave to demonstrate the existence of the discrepancy in the calendar of a world traveler, he suggested a solution. He concludes his discussion of the imaginary journeys of Plato and Socrates in the *Quaestiones supra speram* by observing that:

> From this it follows that if this zone were everywhere habitable, one ought to assign a definite place where a change of the name of the day would be made, for otherwise Socrates would have two names for the same day and the other [Plato] would have the same name for two days.[12]

Even if it is stated in hypothetical terms, here certainly is the practical resolution of the problem: this early proposal of Oresme anticipates by five hundred years the adoption of the International Date Line.

*Part III*

Renaissance Scholarship

6. Beginning of St. Basil's *Address on Reading Greek Literature*

# NOTE ON ST. BASIL'S

## *Address on Reading Greek Literature*

Typical of the medieval attitude toward reading the ancient authors is a story told in the *Life of St. Odo of Cluny* by a contemporary, John of Salerno. Odo, a skillful master of the school of Beaune in the tenth century, as a youth wished to read the poems of Virgil, but he was given a warning to save him from the fatal consequences of such a sinful act. "There was shown him in a vision a certain vessel, most beautiful outside, but full of serpents within. . . . He understood by the serpents the teaching of the poets, by the vessel in which they were contained the book of Virgil; but the way which he had entered so eagerly he understood to be Christ."[1]

If the scholars of the Middle Ages read the learned Latin Fathers, they were certain to be more impressed by St. Jerome's dramatic account of his dream in which he was scourged from Heaven because the Judge declared that he was no Christian but a Ciceronian[2] than they were by St. Augustine's advice in his *De doctrina Christiana*. In that great work on education Augustine says that as the Israelites upon their departure from Egypt, under directions from

Moses, craftily despoiled their captors of their gold and silver, so the Christian should, with good conscience, appropriate from the works of the pagans any passages that he should find true, for he, as a Christian, could put them to better use.[3] Even Augustine's striking statement in his *Confessiones* that he was led to accept the Christian faith chiefly through his reading of Cicero's *Hortensius*[4] seemed to accomplish little in allaying the uneasiness and apprehension concerning reading the ancient heathen writers.[5]

The Italian humanists naturally inherited the medieval prejudice against the pagan writings. To them, moreover, a strong immediate challenge presented itself when the great treasures of Greek literature, unknown but presumably full of pitfalls for the Christian, began to come into Italy after the collapse of the Eastern Empire. Fortunately the Greek scholars who introduced Homer, Hesiod, Euripides, and the rest also brought a small treatise which served as an answer to the humanists' uncertainty about the advisability of reading Greek literature. This was St. Basil's *Address to young men on how they might derive benefit from Greek literature*,[6] a work that had long served Byzantine scholars, and one which was destined to have a profound influence upon education in the West. St. Basil the Great, archbishop of Caesarea (330-379), one of the Greek Fathers most noted for his long struggle to maintain orthodoxy and for his work in establishing monasticism in the East, as well as for his wide learning and humanistic spirit, toward the end of his life wrote this short *Address* to guide young men who were embarking upon the religious life.

Like a wise father who has confidence in the common sense and integrity of his sons, St. Basil treats a sensitive subject in a sane and direct manner. Recognizing their fears that by reading the pagan authors they might jeopardize their very salvation, he reminds the students that the revered and illustrious Moses learned the wisdom of the Egyptians and Daniel studied the teachings of the Chaldeans before they turned to the contemplation of the true God; so, too, he says that the Greek writings hold great truth and wisdom for the Christian. Most of the Greeks were concerned with virtue, but of course they must be read judiciously. When they extol what is good and true and noble, they should be heeded; if ever they teach vice, they should be shunned. In support of his thesis, Basil quotes largely from the poets, Homer, Hesiod, and Theognis, and refers to the teachings of the philosophers and historians, and emphasizes the truth of Prodicus' allegory of the *Choice of Heracles.* He believes that the main benefit to be derived from the study of the ancient authors is moral because they inspire a love of virtue and so prepare the student to understand the great works of the Christian tradition.

Among the Eastern Christians St. Basil's *Address* was widely read, as one may judge by the large number of manuscripts that have been preserved.[7] One of these has been acquired recently by Yale (MS 532). Copied on vellum in a clear hand sometime in the thirteenth century, probably in the Near East, it is now incorporated into a large paper volume of Greek grammatical and rhetorical treatises that were assembled in the mid-sixteenth century. From its contents one must conclude that the volume, comprising well over six hundred folios, was the entire teaching manual of some Greek teacher in Italy. The most notable of the grammatical texts are the works of Constantine Lascaris and Georgios Choeroboskos, the standard grammars for teaching the Greek language. Rhetorical works of Manuel the Rhetorician and Maximus Planudes are included to provide knowledge of composition and effective presentation of one's subject. There are also several literary texts that were commonly used for elementary reading, such as the Orphic Hymns and the Golden Verses of Pythagoras. Finally, the works of the Greek theologians are represented by the letters of Michael Apostolios and Synesius Cyrenaeus and the Dialogue of Theophylactus Simocatta. The teacher who followed this manual successfully would have taught the student how to read and write Greek and how to compose original works. He would have given him practice in reading graduated texts, and finally have introduced him to simple treatises on

Christian theology. St. Basil's *Address* properly has the place of honor at the beginning of the volume, for it is a kind of profession of faith of the teacher and gives direction and encouragement to the student.

Unfortunately not many of the Italian humanists had had such a rigorous course of study and few could read Greek. One of the outstanding exceptions was Leonardo Bruni (1369-1444), who abandoned a career in law to take advantage of the unique opportunity to study Greek under the great Byzantine teacher, Manuel Chrysoloras. To Bruni goes the credit for first making available numerous Greek texts in Latin translations. One of his earliest translations, made in 1402, is St. Basil's *Address* which he calls *De legendis gentilium libris*. For Bruni it was a kind of humanist manifesto. In his dedication to Coluccio Salutati, Bruni says that of all the works of St. Basil, he chose first to make accessible this short treatise because it has a message of the highest import for the scholars of his generation. He says that he hopes by the authority of such a great Christian to crush the perverse prejudice of the narrow-minded people who disparage humanistic studies and think that the ancient authors should be avoided completely.[8] Apparently the treatise was immediately welcomed by scholars, for there are over three hundred manuscript copies of the Latin translation.[9] Of these, two fifteenth-century copies are now in the Yale manuscript collection (MS 179 and Marston MS 105, which has the arms of the Lascaris family). With the coming of printing, Bruni's translation was produced in Venice about 1470, the first of forty-nine editions printed in Italy, Spain, and Germany before 1500.[10]

That Bruni's *De legendis gentilium libris* was welcomed by the early humanists is evidenced by the spirit of freedom and unqualified enjoyment in the ancient literature that generally characterizes their works. One of the first to reflect this new attitude is Bruni himself in a letter addressed to the learned Baptista di Montefeltre, written not long after 1405. Discussing the subject *De studiis et literis*, Bruni speaks of the union of Christian theology with the best in ancient literature as appropriate for the education of women. He concludes by saying, "No (studies) have more urgent claim than the subjects and authors who treat of Religion and of our duties in the world; and it is because they assist and illustrate these supreme studies that I press upon your attention the works of the most approved poets, historians and orators of the past."[11] In the preface to his translation of Plato's *Phaedo* (Marston MS 78) made in 1405, Bruni uses a different argument. In the dedicatory epistle to Pope Innocent VII, he says that in the *Phaedo* Plato approaches so closely to the Christian doctrine of the immortality of the soul that it should serve as a confirmation of that truth. Further, Plato seems to have had some affinity with the true faith; possibly, as others have suggested, he learned this doctrine from the prophet Jeremiah when he was in Egypt, or he may actually have read the Septuagint. Whatever the explanation, Plato's dialogue is salutary study for the Christian.

Aeneas Sylvius Piccolomini (Pope Pius II), a humanist of the generation following Bruni, no longer felt the need to defend his use of classical literature when writing for his own countrymen. But in a treatise entitled *De educatione liberorum,* addressed to Stanislaus, the young king of Bohemia, written in 1450, he invokes the authority of St. Basil on reading the ancient authors, and quotes the *Address* thirteen times. The substance of this work on the education of the prince is taken largely from Plutarch, Quintilian, Cicero, and Sallust, yet there is a recurring statement of precaution. So before a discussion of the poets, he says, "Herein is laid down an admirable principle by which we may be guided in reading all authors of antiquity. Wherever excellence is commended, whether by poet, historian or philosopher, we may safely welcome their aid in building up the character."[12]

In northern Europe Bruni's translation of the *Address* was printed in Germany in 1474, and it was regularly expounded in the University of Paris at the beginning of the sixteenth century. That greatest of all humanists, Erasmus of Rotterdam, edited the Greek text of the works of St. Basil for the Froben press in Basel in 1532.[13] At a time when the Italian humanists had almost lost sight of their original aim of adapting the best elements of classical learning to the enrichment of Christian society, Erasmus, entirely in harmony with St. Basil's counsels on education, devoted many of his writings to the formulation for Christian schools of a meaningful curriculum that would incorporate the noblest thoughts of the ancients into the framework of Christian teachings. In his *Institutio principis Christiani*, written in 1516 for Prince Charles (later Charles V), he expresses the logical conclusion of his theory. He says, "You cannot be a prince, if you are not a philosopher: . . . To be a philosopher and to be a Christian is synonymous in fact."[14] A hundred years later, another Dutch scholar, Hugo Grotius, made a new Latin translation of St. Basil's *Address*, with a commentary,[15] that was printed in Paris in 1623, in Oxford in 1693/4, and again in Frankfort as late as 1688. This would indicate that for over three hundred years since Bruni first made the *Address* available to men of the West, Christian scholars had been seeking justification for their study of the ancient authors in the treatise of that wise Father of the Eastern Church, St. Basil of Caesarea.[16]

# Aesticampianus' Edition

## of the *Tabula* Attributed to Cebes

According to one of his biographers,[1] the chief claim to fame of the German humanist Johannes Rhagius Aesticampianus is the fact that he was the first to introduce the *Tabula (Tablet or Table)* attributed to Cebes to the lands north of the Alps. The time was Easter of the year 1501, and the place, Basel, where Aesticampianus expounded the text to a group of friends.[2] In 1507 his edition of the work, printed by N. Lamperter and B. Murrer, was published in Frankfort, and in 1512 it was reprinted in Leipzig by Jacobus Thanner Herbipolitanus.

Who was this Cebes, the supposed author of a work which played such a prominent role in the career of a distinguished teacher and scholar? The historical Cebes was a citizen of Thebes and a disciple, first of Philolaus the Pythagorean, and then of Socrates. Plato records, in the *Crito* (45B), that Cebes was one of a close group of friends who offered money to help effect Socrates' escape from prison. Again, in the *Phaedo* (59D-63B and *passim*), Plato represents Cebes discussing with Socrates the meaning of death on that last day of

Socrates' life. Legend has it that Cebes purchased Phaedo, who had been a slave, and had him instructed in philosophy.[3] Little else is known of Cebes, but Diogenes Laertius, in his *Lives of the Philosophers* (II, 125), credits him with the authorship of three dialogues, of which no trace has been found; one of these was entitled Πίναξ, the *Tablet*.

By some curious error of identity, a short philosophical work written in the first century A.D. became known as the Πίναξ[4] and was long considered to be the work of Cebes the Theban. Modern critics, basing their conclusions upon the internal evidence of quotations from works of Plato written after Cebes' death and on the presence of late words in the dialogue, are generally agreed that the work could not have been that of Socrates' pupil. This *Tablet* is an allegory of human life in the form of a dialogue. Akin to the early symbolic representation of the two diverse ways of life by the Y of Pythagoras, and to the longer apologue known as the *Choice of Heracles*, which Xenophon reports as the work of Prodicus the Sophist,[5] it is a kind of proto-*Pilgrim's Progress*.

The *Tablet* receives its title from the focal point in the setting of the dialogue. As some visitors are looking at the votive offerings in a temple of Cronos, their attention is attracted to a tablet upon which are depicted numerous strange figures and devices. An old man agrees to explain the meaning of the picture, which he says was dedicated by a philosopher from a foreign land long ago. He then tells them that, in the picture, the circular enclosure with smaller circles inside represents Life, to which a great crowd of people, the unborn, are seeking entrance. At the gate an old man, the Genius or guiding spirit of each individual, offers a scroll with advice to those who are about to enter. Despite this help, the pilgrim setting out on the path of life must endure great temptations and grave dangers as he passes such alluring figures as Deceit, Lust, Avarice, and such awesome personages as Pain, Sorrow, and Despair. Finally, with the aid of Repentance, the wayfarer, though still beset by False Learning, makes for True Doctrine, assisted by Courage and Strength.

7. Cebes' *Tabula*
Aesticampianus' edition of the work, Leipzig, 1512
Beinecke Rare Book and Manuscript Library, Yale University

Eventually he reaches the summit, the radiant meadow of the Blest, where he is welcomed by Knowledge and Happiness, attended by all the Virtues, and is clad in shining garments and crowned with a never-fading garland of flowers. He is then permitted to view the others, who are being held by False Learning and other mistaken values, and he understands that those lives can never find happiness. The whole dialogue is Socratic in spirit as it attempts to show that only by development of his mind by knowledge of the truth and by his attainment of real virtues can man achieve happiness.

Somehow this short Greek dialogue survived the hazards and vicissitudes to which books were subjected during the Middle Ages. Of the thirteen manuscripts that have preserved the text, only two were written before the fifteenth century: one from the eleventh century is now in Paris (MS Parisinus graec. 858), and the other, from the fourteenth century, is in Rome (MS Vaticanus 112). With the revival of interest in the Classics in Italy when the Florentine Academy was endeavoring to recover and study the philosophical tracts associated with Plato and his followers, the Πίναξ received the attention of scholars. Translated into Latin by Ludovicus Odaxius and edited by the illustrious scholar Philip Beroaldus, it was printed in Bologna in 1497.[6] Strangely enough, the first edition of the Greek text, published by Z. Calliergus either in Rome or Venice, seems to have been later: although undated, it is considered to have been printed in 1498. In Venice, Aldus printed an edition of the Greek text with the anonymous translation later used by Aesticampianus in a volume with Lascaris' *Erotemata* in 1501-2 and again in 1512.[7]

During this period of high interest by the Italian humanists in the ancient Greek philosophical works, the German scholar Aesticampianus was studying in Bologna. Having become acquainted with the Latin translation of the            , he introduced it to his circle of learned friends in Basel.[8]

Aesticampianus was one of the first of a class of professors whom one might call international scholars. Born Johannes Rack (Rak) in Sommerfeldt in Lower Lusatia in 1457, he early adopted the name by which he is known to scholarship, Johannes Rhagius Aesticampianus.[9] "Rak" is said to be an old dialectical form meaning "crab," hence the Latinized Greek "Rhagius," while the cognomen "Aesticampianus" was the Latin for his birthplace. Nothing is known of his youth until his matriculation at the University of Cracow in 1491, where he studied under Conrad Celtes. With the recommendation of that very eminent scholar, he went to Vienna in 1499, then to Italy, where he became the pupil of Philip Beroaldus in Bologna. Later, in Rome, he became a friend of Jacob Questenberg and was crowned poet laureate by Pope Alexander VI. His studies and his teaching took him to Basel in 1501, thence to Augsburg, Strassburg, and the University of Mainz. In 1506 he was called to serve as professor of rhetoric and poetry at the University of Frankfort on the Oder. From 1508 to 1510 he lectured on Pliny and Plautus at Leipzig. There one of his students was the erratic genius Ulrich von Hutten, who later recalled in his *Letters of Obscure Men* that Aesticampianus, like Conrad Celtes before him, was driven from the University because the authorities were opposed to the new learning and the fresh approach of the humanists.[10] Aesticampianus' subsequent wanderings took him to Freiburg, where he seems to have been crowned again as poet laureate by the king, to Cracow, to Italy, to be named doctor of theology, to Paris, where he taught Greek, and in 1513 to Cologne. Finally he spent the years from 1517 until his death in 1520 at Wittenberg as professor of Plinian studies.

Aesticampianus was one of the most active and effective of the German humanists. He was also a friend to the leaders of the Reformation movement, Melanchthon and Luther. His extant writings consist of four original works: *Carmina, Epigrammata, Modus epistolandi,* and *Hymnus in laudem Barbarae.* His need for texts in his teaching led him to edit a number of works: the *De grammatica* with a commentary and the *De rhetorica* of Martianus Capella; the *Septem epistolae* of St. Jerome; the *Epistola ad Vespasianum in Libros naturalis historiae* of Pliny; the *Germania* of Tacitus; the *Libellus de vita Christiana* of Saint Augustine; the *De oratore* of Cicero; the *Grammatica* of Petrus Helias; the *Epistolae* of Libanius, and the *Tabula* attributed to Cebes.

By some curious turn of circumstances, none of the larger
works of Aesticampianus engendered so much enthusiasm as
the little dialogue, the *Tabula* attributed to Cebes. His edition
stimulated such a vogue for the work that numerous other
versions and translations into the vernaculars appeared shortly
thereafter. Often it was printed with the *Manual* of Epictetus,
the *Meditations* of Marcus Aurelius, the *Characters* of Theophrastus, or similar works. Of the many editions before the
year 1600,[11] the British Museum now has thirty-six. A translation into English, by Sir Francis Poyntz, was published
about 1530; an Italian translation, by F. A. Coccio, appeared
also in 1530; a Spanish one, by "El doctor poblacion," in
1532; a French one, by G. Corrozet, in 1543; and a German one,
by H. Sachs, in 1570. In 1522 Hans Holbein the Younger made
a large woodcut title border illustrating the *Tablet* for the
title page of Froben's edition of Erasmus' New Testament.
He used the same cut again for the *Geography* of Strabo.[12]

It is to the good fortune of Yale that the Beinecke Library
owns one of the very few known copies of Aesticampianus'
edition of the *Tabula* printed in 1512. It is a slim little book
of only twenty-seven numbered pages, with a full-page
woodcut of the *Tabula* on the title page, apparently copied,
like the text, from the earlier edition of 1507. This woodcut
is less ornate, but in many respects more charming than the
later title-page border of Holbein. The text begins with a
Latin letter from Aesticampianus, "rhetor et poeta laureatus,"
to a beloved pupil, Christopher Ziegler. After complimentary
remarks on the noble family of the young man, he suggests
that in the *Tabula* Christopher will find a mirror of all human
life and lessons to be learned from it. Aesticampianus then
gives a Latin poem in the hendecasyllabic meter, directed
to the reader, which he says he wrote six years earlier (*i.e.*
in 1501) in Basel when he was studying the dialogue with
his friends. There follows the "Argumentum," a summary of
the plot, again addressed to young Ziegler. Still another poem.
an "Epigramma," is also directed to the young man. In it
Aesticampianus gives a Christian orientation to the dialogue
when he says that he has observed in life that nothing is

lasting save virtue, work, and the Grace of Christ, part of which has been indicated in the *Tabula* and part by our free will. The text of the Latin translation of the *Tabula* then follows,[13] and the book ends with an elegiac poem, an exhortation to virtue, by the brilliant young student, Ulrich von Hutten.

The sixteenth century certainly claimed the *Tabula* for its own. Besides the many editions, there was published in Leyden in 1551 another Latin translation by Justus Velsius, who included a 440-page commentary on this "treasury of all moral philosophy." Interest in the work continued to be lively for another century, testified to by the multiplicity of editions[14] and translations into more and more languages. One of the most unusual editions is one prepared by J. Elichmann and published after his death by C. Salmasius in Leyden in 1640: it presents three parallel texts—an Arabic paraphrase, probably of the ninth century; the Latin translation; and the Greek original.[15] Milton, in his famous letter *On Education*, written in 1644, takes the occasion to recommend the study of the *Tablet* as a delightful book to win over the young to a "love of vertue and true labour."[16]

The universal love for allegory was doubtless an important factor in the phenomenal popularity of the dialogue, particularly in northern Europe, for two hundred years after it was first printed. But there is an additional clue, perhaps, in Aesticampianus' epitaph. When one bears in mind that Aesticampianus was a dedicated teacher who loved what he was teaching and who had deep concern and affection for his pupils, then the lines have added significance:

> Rhetoricen, Sophiam, vatum monumenta professus,
> Annis viginti plusve minusve tribus.
> Danubius, Rhenus testatur, et Odera, et Albis,
> Spiraque, cum docta Sequana Gallus aqua.[17]

A man who, as the epitaph states, taught rhetoric, philosophy, and the masterpieces of the poets for twenty-three years in the far-spread territory watered by the Danube, the Rhine, the Oder, the Elbe, and the Seine must have passed on his enthusiasm for the *Tabula* to an uncounted number of students and their students. Would it be sheer fantasy to imagine that this little book might be considered the small pebble that set in motion ever-widening circles of interest in the work?

# Aesticampianus' Commentary

## on the

# *De Grammatica* of Martianus Capella

George Saintsbury, on the occasion of the seventy-fifth birthday of the eminent scholar Dr. Frederick J. Furnivall, wrote a poem to pay tribute to his friend's achievements in philology. It begins:

> *Partes meae sunt quatuor*—Dame Grammar saith, saith she,
> In Martian of the Goatlings (full quaintly writeth he!)
> *Litterae, Litteratura, Litteratus, Litterate!*[1]

In quoting from Martianus Capella, Saintsbury, at the beginning of the twentieth century, was furnishing testimony to the continued relevance of the fifth-century encyclopedia of the seven liberal arts presented in the elaborate allegorical framework of the marriage of Mercury and Philology.[2]

Almost from the start, teachers and scholars had occupied themselves with explaining and annotating the difficult text of Martianus. Long before the ninth century an unnamed commentator branded the author with a moral stricture that actually became incorporated into the text as a colophon in a large number of manuscripts. It reads:

Sic Felix falsus finivit falsa Capella
Corpore qui meruit miseram nunc ducere vitam.[3]

A trio of ninth-century commentators—Martin of Laon, John
the Scot, and Remigius of Auxerre—concentrated first upon
decoding the symbolism of the first two books and considering
the educational implication of the union of speech and
reason;[4] for the other seven books their annotations were
largely synonyms, definitions, paraphrases, or explanations
of difficult passages.[5] This general method of exegesis was
continued in later commentaries and, indeed, persisted even
down to the annotated edition of the youthful Hugo Grotius
in 1599.[6]

It is of some interest, therefore, to find a commentary that
is constructed on quite different principles, one that proposes
to present the substance of the book in simple terms, not
adhering rigidly to the original text, and even introducing
supplementary topics. Yet such is the commentary on the *De
Grammatica* that the German humanist, Johannes Rhagius
Aesticampianus, made in 1508. A year before this book appeared, Aesticampianus had published an edition of Martianus' Book III on grammar[7] for his two nephews for whom
he sought the accomplishments of a Dr. Furnivall. The
little book is adorned with a woodcut depicting Dame Grammar, elegantly dressed for her role, but holding a scalpel and
a file, as well as a long ferule,[8] as she teaches two small boys,
one of whom is carrying a tablet. The preface consists of a
short dedication to "Georgi et Iohannes nepotes mei charis-
simi." The Martianus text, which includes only the actual
material on grammar without the allegorical setting, is followed by an elegiac poem by Ulric von Hutten (who was once
a student of Aesticampianus) in the form of an exhortation
to the boys to study the liberal arts.[9]

Apparently Martianus' *Grammatica* must have proved too
difficult for the young students because Aesticampianus soon
published his *Commentarii*[10] for their assistance. The
printer of his second little book used the same woodcut of
Grammar with her pupils. In his introductory epistle to the

8. Dame Grammar and her pupils
Aesticampianus' Commentary on the *De Grammatica* of
Martianus Capella, Frankfort, 1508
Sächsische Landesbibliothek, Dresden

nephews, the author speaks of the *obscuritas* and *ieiunitas* of Martianus' style, serious defects that Saintsbury had charitably referred to in his adverb 'quaintly'; he suggests that other students also might find it useful to have some explanations of the technical terminology and fuller discussion of some of the topics.[11] The commentary makes no reference to the allegorical setting. While it uses the Martianus text as background, the material is organized somewhat independently, with elaborations of some topics, omissions of others, and, at the end, two large topics from Donatus. The text of the commentary is printed in Gothic type, digressions of the commentator and quotations from other sources are in roman type, and *lemmata* from Martianus are in roman capitals.

The commentary begins with the basic elements of the discipline of grammar, the alphabet—*litterae*—the first of Martianus' four parts of grammar. Very aptly Aesticampianus quotes the verses of Manilius in which the poet emphasizes the importance of the letters as the foundation of poetry.[12] He then defines the letter, gives its etymology, and cites its properties, names, forms, and pronunciation. Although the Martianus text deals at length with the individual letters of the Latin alphabet, there is no discussion of the origin of the alphabet. Aesticampianus, naming his authorities as Herodotus, Suidas, Pliny, Tacitus, and Rufus Festus, presents the theories of the beginnings of the alphabet in Syria or in Egypt. He notes its transference to Greece and the addition of letters by Cecrops, Palamedes, and Epicharmus; he remarks upon the introduction of the Greek letters into Italy by Saturn or by Evander; he comments upon the three letters that Claudius endeavored to add to the Latin alphabet.[13] He concludes with a six-line poem that he says occurs "in priscis monumentis." Because of the mention of Ulfilas, it seems worth noting.

> Moyses primus Hebraicas exaravit litteras;
> Mente Phoenices sagaci condiderunt Atticas.
> Quas Latini scriptitamus edidit Nicostrata.
> Abraham Syras et idem repperit Caldaicas.

Isis arte non minori protulit Aegyptias.
Gulfila prompsit Getarum quas videmus ultimas.[14]

Aesticampianus adds several items of interest beyond what Martianus had treated upon the subject of letters. For instance, he discusses the letter *Y*, the letter of Pythagoras,[15] at some length, and quotes the line of Martial's epigram that refers to its invention by Palamedes from observing the flight of cranes.[16] Again, commenting upon the letter *R*, Aesticampianus notes that the Latin language does not aspirate it, as the Greeks do, when it is the initial letter of a word.[17] To the information on the letter *T*, he adds the common observation that the Greek letter resembles the sign of the Cross.[18] For all of the letters he gives abundant examples from Latin literature.

The second of Martianus' "partes" is *litteratura*, which Grammatica defines as "ipsa quae doceo," that is, the study of formal grammar. This includes consideration of the syllable, accent, noun, pronoun, adverb, conjunction, preposition, interjection, and verb, all of which constitute the general category of *analogia*, the regular forms. There follows a very brief account of *anomala*, the irregularities. In elucidating this section, Aesticampianus first defines grammar as "ars liberalis que usu et experientia prompta omne genus scriptionis latine perpendit ac dijudicat, ne loquutionis scriptureve vitio aliquo inquinetur riteque pronuncietur, poetarum oratorumque atque historicorum sensus tenet atque exarat."[19] He comments upon Quintilian's division of grammar into two parts,[20] and discusses Cicero's theories of the function of grammar.[21] He quotes Varro's fourfold division of grammar—*lectio, enarratio, emendatio,* and *iudicium*[22]—and contrasts it with Martianus' fourfold division which apparently he finds inadequate, perhaps because he finds Donatus' treatment more logical.[23] He then affirms that grammar is, indeed, divided into four parts: *littera, syllaba, dictio* and *oratio*.[24] Yet, in general, he follows his author in the topics he treats, but he always illustrates his points with many examples. In instances where he finds Martianus' explanations deficient, he fills in. So, after explaining the tenses, he says that Martianus omitted consideration of the supine, and then he gives his own treatment of the subject.[25] Again, Martianus simply states that impersonal constructions do occur; Aesticampianus adds a section: "De constructione impersonalium extra authorem."[26] At the end of Martianus' treatment of all regular forms, *analogia,* Aesticampianus adds a section on *De constructione,* lest, he tells the nephews, the whole structure of discourse collapse.[27] In this part, it is interesting to note that the commentator, who had hitherto been quite impersonal now speaks in the first person, giving his name and examples from the current situation of his teaching grammar to the two young men.[28] Returning to Martianus' brief paragraph on *anomala,* he enlarges the topic with many illustrations.

Martianus' third part of grammar, *litteratus,* after the initial definition "quem docuero,"[29] was given scant attention by Martianus himself, and then only incidentally. Here one finds great divergence in Aesticampianus, as one observes chiefly in his manner and attitude throughout the commentary. First of all, to define grammar he quotes a long passage from Suetonius' *De grammaticis*[60] where he cites Cornelius Nepos to the effect that the common understanding of *litteratus* is an educated person who speaks or writes carefully, accurately, and intelligently. He also gives definitions of Cicero and Quintilian. One has the impression that this aspect of grammar had great importance in the estimation of the commentator. Obviously Aesticampianus himself knows Latin literature thoroughly. Having been a teacher his whole life, he expects his students to have wide knowledge of that field. Hence he can mention without specific reference to Terence, the famous line "Davos sum, non Oedipus."[31] and refer to Virgil's epitaph, "Mantua me genuit . . . ,"[32] with the assurance that it will be recognized. In illustrating the various points of grammar, he quotes Virgil more than eighty times, Plautus and Cicero each more than thirty times, Juvenal twenty-five, Ovid and

Pliny each twenty times, Lucretius and Horace each fifteen. There are numerous citations from Terence, Varro, Sallust, Livy, Persius, Martial, Lucan, Statius, and Suetonius. Several come from Ennius, Cato, Pacuvius, Catullus, Columella, Aulus Gellius, Macrobius, and Servius. Occasional references are made to Apuleius, St. Augustine, Eusebius, Probus, Hieronymus, Diomedes, Priscian, Charisius, and Festus. Many of these must, of course, have come to the commentator at second hand. There are a few rather unusual quotations from Serenus Sammonicus,[33] St. Cyprianus,[34] and Papyrianus.[35] The only Renaissance work he quotes is Lorenzo Valla's *Elegantiae*.[36]

The second way in which Aesticampianus shows his concern for the education of the *litteratus* is his introduction of biographies of literary personages, when he finds an opportunity. He gives, for example, information concerning the life of Catullus along with two quotations from his poems.[37] For Lucretius he repeats the biographical details supplied by Eusebius.[38] The lives of Sallust,[39] Virgil,[40] Accius,[41] Lucilius,[42] and the two Licinii[43] are given briefer notice. He also expects his students to have some familiarity with the common Greek myths. In addition to a quantity of single-word references, he makes more extended comments on Ariadne, Orpheus, Jason, Pelops, Phaethon, and Helen. He assumes that his students have some elementary knowledge of Greek, for he uses Greek words frequently in etymologies. He refers to incidents in Homer, and mentions Pindar, Plato, Aristotle, Theocritus, and Aristarchus. Quite naturally he thinks of the *litteratus* as *Christianus*, as he uses many Biblical names such as Daniel, Michael, Raphael, Joachim, Jacob, Ruth, David, and Abraham. He quotes Augustine's statement that Hebrew, Greek, and Latin are necessary for an understanding of Holy Scripture.[44]

Only at the end of his commentary on Martianus' *De Grammatica*, in a kind of appendix, does Aesticampianus make reference to the allegorical setting of his author, when he addresses his nephews. Here he paraphrases Martianus' statement that Grammar had more topics to expound but

that Apollo forced her to conclude her speech as he introduced the next bridesmaid, Rhetorica.[45] Some of the subjects that Grammar had expected to treat were thus given to
Rhetorica to explain. Aesticampianus tells his students that
he intends—God willing—to elucidate this art also with
commentaries which they would do well to read.[46] Two of
the subjects that Grammar was most reluctant to omit were
key points in Martianus' fourth division of grammar,
*litterate*, that is skillfully and correctly applying the rules to
speech. These two topics, *soloecismorum causae* and *barbarae
formae* (grammatical errors and improprieties of speech),
were subjects the commentator also considered essential to
any discussion of grammar. Hence Aesticampianus forthwith
added a section *De barbarismo* and *De soloecismo*, indicating
that he was here following the text of Donatus.[47] He does
adhere quite consistently to the treatment of Donatus, while
enlarging upon some points and always giving plenty of
examples. He also comments on Donatus' *De ceteris vitiis*,
but he observes that Donatus' clear and succinct discussion of
*De metaplasmo* leaves nothing to be added.[48]

At the very end Aesticampianus again addresses the
nephews, exhorting them to study his commentary while
their minds are at ease and their fortune secure, and they enjoy God's help.[49]

After the commentary, a poetic conceit in the form of a
thirty-five-line poem, purporting to have been written by
the Muses of Aesticampianus, gives the time and place of
the composition.[50] It was written in the author's forty-fifth
year, in a city on the banks of the Oder, that is, Frankfort.
The work has served as a solace for the writer's misfortune
and a source of comfort to the persecuted scholar who is
forced to leave his family, his friends, and his beloved native
land. The Muses bid the boys return to Lusatia while they,
on the other hand, will follow the old scholar into exile:

> Quo vel fata vocent deus vel author
> Vel fors hac melior schola vel urbe.[51]

A second poem by the Muses, this time addressed to the reader, calls attention to Aesticampianus' service as interpreter in clearing away with his sickle the thorny brambles of Martianus' tortured style that made it difficult to understand his grammar.[52] The Muses then convey to the reader the author's invitation to climb the lofty heights where Philology and her maidens dwell, in the company of the Lusatian nephews.

Lusatia, the homeland of Aesticampianus, was always dear to the heart of the scholar; he once wrote a long poem in her honor. This elegy was sent by Melanchthon to Frobenius in Basel to be printed, but somehow, most unfortunately, it was lost and never recovered. The incident is related by Christopher Manlius,[53] a fellow countryman who, in his work on the famous men of Lusatia, wrote Aesticampianus' biography some thirty years after the scholar's death.[54] Here, and in subsequent accounts,[55] one find the essential facts concerning his career. Johannes Rhagius Aesticampianus Lusatus, *Doctor Theologus, Rhetor et Poeta laureatus praecellens, vir honestissimus et doctissimus*, was born Johannes Rack (Rhagius) in the little town of Sommerfeld (Aesticampianus) in Lower Lusatia (Lusatus) in East Germany in the year 1457. He studied under Conrad Celtes at the University of Cracow in 1491, then in Vienna in 1499, in Bologna as a pupil of Philip Beroaldus, and finally in Rome where he was crowned poet laureate by Pope Alexander VI. He was called to teach in Basel in 1501, then shortly after in Augsburg, and in Strassburg, and as Professor of Moral Philosophy at the University of Mainz until 1505. The following year he was called to his homeland to become Professor of Rhetoric and Poetics at the University of Frankfort on the Oder. There he also taught Greek to a large number of students. In 1508, with his pupil Ulric von Hutten, he went to the University of Leipzig. Dismissed from this post after three years by the reactionary officials at the University, he next taught at Freiberg where Petrus Mosellanus became his assistant, and he received a second crown as poet laureate from the Emperor Maximilian.

From Freiberg  he went to Italy,  and in 1513 to Cologne. In 1517 he went to Wittenberg where he lectured on Pliny. There he died in 1520 and was honored in the parish church by a bronze plaque inscribed with a long epitaph enumerating his achievements.[56]

Aesticampianus' scholarly works reflect his interest in teaching. He prepared editions of the *Septem Epistolae* of St. Jerome, the *Libellus de vita Christiana* of St. Augustine, Pliny's *Epistola ad Vespasianum in Libros naturalis historiae*, Cicero's *De oratore*, Tacitus' *Germania*, Petrus Helias' *Grammatica* with a commentary, the *Epistolae* of Libanius, the *Tabula* of Cebes, the *De Rhetorica* of Martianus Capella, and the *De Grammatica* with a commentary. There are also four original works: *Hymnus in laudem Barbarae, Modus epistolandi, Carmina,* and *Epigrammata.*

One of the German humanists, Aesticampianus was associated in one way or another with many of the scholars of his day: Conrad Celtes, Vincentius Longinus, Philip Beroaldus, Jacob Questenberg, Jacob Wimpheling, Conrad Wimpina, Ulric von Hutten, Herman von dem Busche, Johann Reuchlin, Petrus Mosellanus, Philip Melanchthon, and Martin Luther.

*Part IV*

# Bishop Dubravius, Bohemian Humanist

# Bishop Dubravius

## on Fishponds

Of late I tooke my lodging in a Towne neare unto the Alpes called Aenipontus [Innsbruck], and desired mine Hoast to prepare Troutes to my supper. Mine Hoast answered againe, Sir, if you love Fish well, I will shew you a better and a sweeter Fish then is a Troute, and with that without any delay he brought me Carpes, not long before brought out of Bohemia, praysing and extolling them to the uttermost: sometimes comparing them to the Carpes bredde in the lake Garde, and sometimes with Salmons of the Rheyne. (Leaf 35 recto)

The innkeeper could not have pleased his guest more, for he was entertaining a native of Bohemia who was also a connoisseur of fish, Janus Dubravius, at that time secretary to Bishop Stanislaus Thurzo of Olmütz. The incident is related by Dubravius in a book that was written in Latin and published in Breslau in 1547, then translated into English at the special request of George Churchey, Fellow of Lions Inn, and printed at London by William White, "dwelling in Cowlane," in 1599.[1] The English title gives a good impres-

sion of its contents and purpose: *A New Booke Of good Husbandry, very pleasant, and of great profite both for Gentlemen
and Yomen: Conteining, The Order and maner of making
of Fish-pondes, with the breeding, preserving, and multi-
plying of the Carpe, Tench, Pike, and Troute, and diverse
kindes of other Fresh-fish.* The sponsor of the English
translation, in a letter to the reader, states that he had the
work published "for that it is so necessarie for a Common-
wealth." Because our own generation, too, regards the whole
subject of ecology as urgent for the entire society, it has
seemed relevant to recall the prudent sixteenth-century bishop
of Olmütz.

Janus Dubravius (1486-1533), lawyer, Classical scholar,
historian, and Churchman, cherished throughout his life a
deep love for his troubled Bohemia and a simple devotion to
the land. Every aspect of husbandry interested him and he
contemplated writing treatises on a number of areas in the
general field,[2] but his official duties, first as assistant to
Bishop Thurzo and then as Bishop of Olmütz, kept him from
accomplishing his purpose. The one part of the work that he
did finish, the book on fishponds and fish, was begun at the
request and with the aid of Bishop Thurzo, but was dis-
continued when the Bishop died. Eventually, after constant
reminders by his friends that as spiritual heir to the fishermen
apostles Thomas and Peter he had an obligation to finish the
book, he completed it as a memorial to his former bishop.

For Dubravius the culture of fish was not simply theoretical.
In his dedicatory letter to Anton Fugger,[3] nephew and heir
to the German financier Jakob Fugger, he recalls an interesting episode that illustrates his personal experience with
the subject. Fugger once invited him for a visit to his newly
acquired estate in Pannonia, land that had in the thirteenth
century belonged to Constance, Queen of Bohemia, wife
of Ottakar I. He found the grounds and buildings completely neglected as a result of the avarice of a later owner.
Fugger determined to spare neither money nor effort to
restore the place, and Dubravius immediately begged for
the opportunity of overseeing the reclamation of the fishponds.

The little treatise on fishponds and fish is no casual essay but a systematic treatment of the subject. Though it was written for Bohemia, it applies equally well to other countries. For his authorities Dubravius quotes all the Roman writers on agriculture, but chiefly Varro, Vitruvius, and Columella, on the location, construction, and care of ponds and the propagation of fish, while he cites Pliny and Ausonius on the nature and varieties of fish. He always treats his restricted subject in relation to the whole field of husbandry. After an introduction in which he speaks of the antiquity of making fishponds, the various types of ponds, and the kinds of fish suitable for propagation, he treats in detail (1) the situation, placing, and construction of ponds, (2) the means of conveying water into them, (3) the duties and offices of a pond-keeper, and (4) the times for fishing, and the instruments pertaining to the same.

The practical information Dubravius furnished in his treatise must have been of particular usefulness to large land-owners of the sixteenth and seventeenth centuries because his was the only work on the subject since Roman times: the Italian scholar Pietro Crescenzi in 1306 had written a *Ruralia commoda*,[4] which was translated into several languages; the Englishmen Walter of Henley in the thirteenth century and Anthony Fitzherbert in the sixteenth wrote books on husbandry; but none of these included sections on fishponds. Dubravius' work quickly became so popular that it went through seven editions.

Today the book is of interest because of what one may consider its modern approach to the problems of environmental protection. This concern for preserving the natural features of the surroundings can be seen in several aspects of the treatise. In the first place, the author takes a long-range view of his subject. On the matter of planning for a fishpond he advises the landowner to make the important initial decisions as to the location of the pond only after he has surveyed his holdings with a view to the prevalence of sunshine and shade, type of soil, accessibility to a source of running water, and the possibilities for good drainage, to determine the most healthful situation for usefulness year after year. His second consideration is the actual preparation of the pond. This must be done in a scientific way with regard for the optimum size, given the needs of the owner, the best possible means of taking advantage of the natural features in building a dam and sluice gates, the most effective ways of providing banks and hedges to protect the pond from intruders, whether cattle or predators, and devices for regulating the water. Again the advice of the expert is suggested for the culture of the fish, including their propagation, the nursery for the young fry, the feeding of the fish and the treatment of their diseases, and the methods for keeping the pond clean and free from weeds. He also gives instructions for proper harvesting of the fish; that is, when, how many, and how often fish should be taken from the ponds in order to maintain a flourishing colony that can be expected to serve the owner indefinitely. Finally he warns that ponds must be "renewed and refreshed" every eight or nine years; the fish must be moved to another area so that the pond can be drained completely and kept free of water for a year; but corn can be sown in the rich silt of the bottom.[5]

Besides these technical concerns, the treatise contains other matters of general interest. For example, Dubravius indicates that a fishpond properly constructed and cared for not only assures financial gain to the owner, but affords whatever pleasant experiences derive from fishing. Like the English Dame Juliana Berners, who in her essay *On Fishing with an Angle*[6] endeavored to elevate fishing to a gentleman's sport comparable to hunting and hawking, Dubravius sought to give the occupation the prestige of noble or royal patronage. After relating how a governor of Silesia when caught fishing justified his action as no more unfit or unbecoming than hunting, he tells (leaf 2 recto) of the elegant and cultured King Matthias of Hungary (1440-90):

Mathias king of Hungarie was not ashamed often times to bayte at Pond-yardes: and when as almost all the Kinges which raigned before him in Hungarie, had wonne great renowne through their valiant deedes, hee found the meanes by the great magnificence of Pondes, to excell in prayse the most commendable and worthiest Fish maisters in Bohemia.

It is interesting to note that Robert Burton, in suggesting fishing as a remedy for melancholy, cites this incident in Dubravius to show that fishing is entirely suitable for a gentleman.[7]

Like many another fishing enthusiast, Dubravius has a stock of good fish stories which he relates with a humorous touch. He tells, for instance, of a duel between a frog and a pike (leaf 5 verso):

> I can not choose, but must needes in this place commit to wryting that spectacle which once I saw with mine eyes at the Pondes nigh to the Castle Cremsiris, when as I accompanied Byshop Stanislane Thurzo: There lay lurking in a corner of the Pondes side a Frogge at variance with a Pike . . . .

As they watch, the frog and the fish put on a jousting match which lasts for a long time until the pike is forced to the bottom, blinded and disabled (leaf 6 recto).

> . . . beholde sodaynly the Frogge riseth to the toppe, reioycing and crooking like a conquerour, getteth him againe to his cave.

The Bishop had to have the conquered pike rescued and removed from the scene. (That prince of all fishermen, Izaak Walton, reports that when he repeated this story to a friend, the reply was, "It was as improbable as to have the mouse scratch out the cat's eyes.")[8]

One of his best stories is a concrete demonstration of the need for his book (leaf 14 recto):

> Of late a certaine Knight of Bohemia . . . going about to winne the goodwill of a ritch olde Widdow, he bragged & vaunted his knowledge to be as good in making of Pondes, as in debating of matters: and for a tryall of his cunning, he

digged in that place a Ponde, whereto no kinde of water or moysture might be brought. This his deede caused him to be a sufficient laughing stocke: yet he exagarated his folly more with his wordes, in that he defended it, and reasoned of the filling of this Ponde, not by gourdes of raine water, but by a miraculous manner, as by such a miracle as is mentioned in Moses booke.

For his double foolishness he was forsaken and rejected by the rich widow. Clearly he should have read Dubravius' book and learned how to make fishponds properly.

# A DIAMOND AND A DÜRER IN DUBRAVIUS'
## COMMENTARY ON MARTIANUS CAPELLA

> I had a whisper from a ghost, who shall be nameless, that
> these commentators always kept in the most distant quarters
> from their principals in the lower world, through a conscious-
> ness of shame and guilt, because they had so horribly misrep-
> resented the meaning of those authors to posterity.
>
> *(Gulliver's Travels,* III.8)

Jonathan Swift thus harshly condemned commentators
because he felt that they distorted and even falsified their
authors' works. A commoner charge against them is that they
are frequently uncreative, unimaginative pedants who produce dull, often irrelevant masses of material that sometimes
even further clouds the original text. A scholar would seem
to be inviting adverse criticism in choosing to write about
a work that is itself already controversial. The *De nuptiis
Mercurii et Philologiae* (On the Marriage of Mercury and
Philology) of Martianus Capella is such a book. The
fifth-century writer's great encyclopedia was responsible for
fixing the pattern of education in the mold of the seven
liberal arts for eight centuries and has been called the most

successful textbook ever written; yet it has also been branded variously as detestable in style, obscure in meaning, and sterile in content. The Bohemian scholar Janus Dubravius was therefore accepting an obvious risk in writing a Latin commentary on the first two allegorical books of Martianus Capella's work. Happily, his commentary belies the critics. A man of wide learning and an original turn of mind, Dubravius wrote a treatise that does not misinterpret the author, presents material pertinent to an understanding of the text, and further undertakes to outline a universal application of the allegory.

Dubravius (Jan Dubraw), a prominent humanist, achieved distinction as Churchman, historian, and pioneer conservationist. Born in Pilsen in 1486, he was originally named Skala, but he early assumed the more honored name of Dubrausky from an old branch of the family in Moldavia. He studied in Italy, where he earned the degree of Doctor of Laws. Back in Bohemia, he assumed the duties of administrative assistant to Stanislaus, Bishop of Olmütz. He himself served as Bishop of Olmütz from 1546 until his death in 1553. His chief scholarly work is a great history of Bohemia, *Historia regni Boiemiae*, first published in Prossnitz by Joannes Guntherus in 1552 and often reprinted. In quite different fields, he wrote a long poem entitled *Theriobulia* upon the accession of Louis II to the throne of Bohemia (printed in Nuremberg in 1520), and a commentary on Psalm V (published in Prossnitz in 1549). The work of his that is best known outside of Bohemia, a scientific treatise on fishponds and fish, *De piscinis et piscium qui in eis aluntur naturis*, was first printed in Breslau in 1547. This book, translated into English for George Churchey and published in London in 1599, was widely used in England by large landowners interested in preserving their natural resources.

Dubravius' commentary on the allegory of Martianus Capella, written when he was a young scholar recently returned from Italy where he had become absorbed in the intellectual pursuits of the humanists, was published in Vienna by H. Vietor in 1516.[1] The least known of his writings, it deserves study. It is prefaced by a long dedicatory epistle to Bishop Stanislaus Thurzo, and at the end there is a gracious letter of acknowledgment from the Bishop. The commentary appears not to have been written for young students, like some of the earlier books on the *De nuptiis*, but rather for mature readers. Dubravius does not concern himself with the minutiae of words, phrases, and definitions, but instead with giving the overall meaning of the allegory. His method is to quote a short paragraph of Martianus and then discuss the ideas put forth in the passage, endeavoring to find some universal application of his author's cosmic marriage of reason and speech, the basis of philosophy.

In his commentary, Dubravius shows himself to be an accomplished scholar of the Classics, quoting from more than sixty Greek and Latin authors, making numerous references to Greek and Roman history and literature. He also cites several Renaissance writers. Amid all of these scholarly references, two allusions to contemporary phenomena, of which he was an eyewitness, are of more than usual interest, especially since they appear to have gone unnoticed. One refers to a magnificent diamond that belonged to Jacob Fugger in Augsburg, and the other to a splendid painting by Dürer that hung in the Bishop's palace in Breslau.

In discussing Martianus Capella's naming of the twelve precious gems that symbolize the zodiac, Dubravius adds a personal comment (on page 104). Translated from his Latin, it reads:

> Recently in the very grand city of Augsburg, there was shown to me by Jacob Fugger, a most cultured man and one of the most refined taste in the more elegant luxuries, a diamond such as Pliny and Solinus describe as being found among the peoples of India. It was the size of a walnut, of the greatest purity and highest brilliance, shaped like a double cone, with six sides, tapering to a point at each end. After I had gazed in admiration at the diamond for quite a long time, I ventured to ask what value he would place upon such extremely rare treasures of nature. He replied that, if he had to part with the diamond, he would not exchange it for less than one hundred thousand gold

florins. Let it be said, begging the kind indulgence of the
kings, that not a single ruler in our age would possess such
great riches concentrated in such a small object.

Now, assuming the role of commentator upon a commentator,
I should like to note, in corroboration of the story, that (a)
as a young man in the service of Bishop Stanislaus Thurzo,
Dubravius must have visited Jacob Fugger in Augsburg; (b)
the great Fugger commercial empire frequently dealt in
precious stones; and (c) a contemporary Italian diary records
the circumstances under which Jacob Fugger received a most
unusual diamond.[2]

In 1494 the firm of Ulrich Fugger and Brothers entered
upon a partnership with the Thurzo Company of Cracow,
headed by Johann Thurzo. This very successful combination
of the vast German trading enterprise with the great Hungarian
mining industry was the foundation of the Fuggers' financial
empire and the extraordinary personal fortune of Jacob
Fugger.[3] The business relationship was further strengthened
by two important marriages between the Fugger family and
the Thurzo: in 1497 Anna Fugger, daughter of Ulrich,
married George Thurzo, and in 1513 Raymund Fugger, son
of George, married Katharina Thurzo.[4] In another area, the
Church, three grandsons of Johann Thurzo attained high
position. Of these, Stanislaus, as Bishop of Olmütz, had great
influence upon the secular as well as the religious life of
his people. Since the Fugger-Thurzo finances played a large
role in underwriting some of the activities of the Church,
Dubravius, as assistant to the Bishop, must on occasion have
been sent to Augsburg to the Fuggers on official business.
It was, then, on one of these visits, that he was shown the
great diamond. Apparently Dubravius continued on friendly
personal relations with the Fugger family, for in 1547 he
dedicated his book on fishponds and fish to Anton Fugger,
nephew and chief heir to Jacob.[5]

The great financial monopoly of the Fuggers, conspicuous
for its backing of the princes of the Church and the rulers
of Europe, resulted, of course, from their earlier control of
the mineral resources of the Continent, particularly copper,

gold, and silver.[6] Extensive records of their business transactions reveal that precious stones also were sometimes used
as a medium of exchange, though these often took their
place among the treasures of the Fugger mansion. It is known,
for example, that some of the extraordinary pieces of jewelry
that Charles the Bold of Burgundy lost at the time of his
defeat at Grandson at the hands of the Swiss in 1476 eventually
came into the possession of Jacob Fugger.[7] It is probably
from this source that he received an unusually fine single
diamond, the size of half a walnut.[8] There is also a record
of a diamond circlet, worth 29,800 ducats, that Fugger
acquired in August 1516 from the Pisani Bank in Venice,
an amazing piece of jewelry that had earlier adorned the
head-dress of a sultan in Egypt.[9]

It is not without precedent, therefore, that in 1509 Jacob
Fugger received a magnificent diamond from a banking
firm in Venice that had undergone bankruptcy. The episode
is related in the diary of a Venetian scholar, Marino
Sanuto, in his entry for 14 April 1509.[10] He reveals that
the Agostini bank, which owed Jacob Fugger for 500,000
pounds of copper, resolved their obligation by delivering
to Fugger's agent a large diamond valued at 20,000 gold
ducats. This would appear to be the magnificent solitaire
that Dubravius saw in Augsburg. One of Fugger's modern
biographers (who gives no indication of having seen the
Dubravius reference), remarking upon the great cost of this
gem, says that never once did the Hungarian royal couple,
who were famous for their extravagance in jewelry, venture
to indulge in such a luxury.[11] (Undoubtedly he refers to
the elegant Matthias Corvinus and his beautiful wife,
Beatrice of Naples.)

It is ironical that Jacob Fugger kept his prized diamond,
"einer Sensation jener Zeit," for just one year. Sanuto, in his
diary for 30 May 1510 (X,283), records that Pope Julius II
bought the diamond for 18,000 ducats and wore it, with other
jewels, on his cope. Why Fugger sold the gem and why he
took a loss of 2,000 ducats are questions that no one has been
able to answer. Certainly few are satisfied with the popular

theory that he sold it to avoid arousing the envy of the nobles and the ill will of the people. The shrewd financial wizard and manipulator of dynasties must have exchanged his cherished diamond for greater gains.[12] The eventual disposition of the diamond remains unknown. It is possible that when Pope Julius II died on 21 February 1513, his precious cope was interred with him.[13] Another possibility is that, along with a papal tiara, it went back to the Agostini bank in settlement of the Pope's debts. What is of real interest is that Dubravius has given us the only extant description of the famous gem by a person who had actually seen it.

Dubravius' second personal reference to a contemporary phenomenon of interest occurs in a passage in the Commentary where he is assessing the great accomplishments of the Greeks in the graphic arts. He remarks that, in painting, modern artists are not to be considered less skilled than the ancients, and to substantiate his claim writes (on page 77):

> I have recently seen a picture painted by one Albert of German nationality, which, so far as I myself am able to judge (and painters confirm my opinion), is of the most exquisite perfection. In this picture Adam and Eve are depicted, nude and standing figures. They are looking up, in wonder, with lips parted and eyes widened, at a tree at this time still pleasing to them. The faces of both are noble, rosy, even blushing; their hair is golden yellow and seemingly blown back by a breeze; their eyes are bluish-gray and sparkling. Finally, in each there is a natural beauty of body that the artist has succeeded in depicting by preserving the remarkable difference in their nature and sex, for he has represented Adam with wide shoulders and a manly chest, while in Eve he has emphasized the waist and hips. All other parts of their bodies are in such exact harmony that there is not the slightest imperfection. They say, indeed, that the painter exercised such care and took such trouble (no doubt following Zeuxis) that when he was going to paint the picture, he used to go to the public baths where the body is customarily exposed, in order to reproduce in his painting what he found most praiseworthy in each body. Nor did this zeal of his go unrewarded, for Joannes Thurzo, Bishop of Breslau, who will always be considered among my chief pa-

trons, a man of great nobility and excellent taste, bought the
painting from the artist for one hundred and twenty gold
florins. He hung the picture in his chamber, and there it
catches the attention not only of princes and most noble guests,
but also challenges the hands of painters and sculptors to
imitate it.

Here the commentator on the Commentary is confronted
by an enigma: Where is this picture? It is well known that
Dürer was long fascinated by the theme of the Fall of Man,
for at least thirteen preliminary studies on the subject still
exist,[14] and two of his major works depict Adam and Eve.
One is a large engraving of the pair standing one on either
side of a tree.[15] A snake, coiled over one of the branches, is
offering the apple which Eve is about to receive. Adam's left
hand is extended toward Eve, while his right holds a branch
on which a parrot is perched and from which hangs a label,
"Albertus Durer Noricus faciebat 1504," and the monogram.
A series of animals in repose fills the foreground and the
background. The other representation is a life-sized painting
on two separate panels, possibly made for two sides of an
altar piece.[16] Both figures are painted against dark back-
grounds, without animals or birds, and the tree is on the far
side of Eve. Adam is holding a small branch with an apple;
Eve is taking the apple from the serpent twined around the
tree trunk. A label on a small branch in Eve's right hand
bears the inscription: "Albertus Durer Alemanus faciebat
post Virginis partum 1507" and the monogram. These panels
once belonged to Queen Christina of Sweden and are now in
the Prado in Madrid. There are two copies of the group, one
in the Altertumsmuseum in Mainz and the other in the Pitti
Palace in Florence. (It is interesting to note that in the second
copy there are animals and birds in the background.)
Dürer painted the Adam and Eve panels shortly after his
sojourn in Venice, where he had occupied himself particularly with studying the proportions of the human body and
with painting nude figures. That he succeeded admirably in
both objectives is indicated by the universal praise that

critics have given the representations of Adam and Eve.
The earliest judgment appears to have been made in several
short poems, published in 1522, by the historian and poet
Caspar Ursinus Velius. Of these, one Latin distich may be
translated :

> When the angel saw them, marvelling, he said, "I should
> not have driven such beautiful people from Paradise."[17]

What is the relationship between the Prado panels and
the painting of Adam and Eve that Dubravius described? One
must say immediately that the latter is not the original of
which the Prado group is a copy, nor is it a copy of the Prado
picture, for the two differ in composition. The picture Dubravius saw was a single painting rather than two panels,
and the two people depicted were standing one on either
side of the tree. The varied history of the Prado panels from
the time they were placed in the Rathaus in Nuremberg in
1507, thence to Prague, to Venice, and to Spain, is fairly well
documented. There is no indication they were ever in Breslau.
On the other hand, Dubravius says that Bishop Joannes
Thurzo bought his painting from Dürer for 120 gold florins
and that he hung it in his palace. We learn further from one
of Dürer's own letters, dated 4 November 1508, that the
Bishop bought another painting, "Madonna with the Iris,"
long at Prague, but now in Richmond, England, for 72 gold
florins.[18]

Unless Dubravius' account is to be discredited, one is
bound to conclude that there were two original paintings
of Adam and Eve, one divided into two panels, now in the
Prado, and the other, a single composition, that was sold
to Joannes Thurzo and taken immediately to Silesia. The
fact that this painting left Germany so promptly may
account for the curious situation of none of the early biographers' seeming to have known of its existence. The noted
art critic, Joachim von Sandrart, in his account of Dürer in
1675, simply records that the artist painted a life-sized Adam
and Eve in 1507[19] The sole reference that I have found that
may pertain to the Breslau painting is a bare statement, with
no indication of source, made by one of the leading modern

critics, Hans Tietze, that in the seventeenth century there was a copy of the Adam and Eve painting in the possession of the Archbishop of Olmütz.[20] This could well have been the Breslau painting, since Joannes Thurzo, Archbishop of Breslau in the early sixteenth century, was the brother of Stanislaus Thurzo, Archbishop of Olmütz. One is left to conclude, however, that the work has been lost. Must this, then, be the unsatisfactory ending to the story of the discovery of the painting in Dubravius' Commentary? Must one accept as final that Dürer's splendid painting of Adam and Eve, once the showpiece of the Archbishop's palace in Breslau, is no longer in existence?

# THE *Theriobulia*

## OF JAN DUBRAVIUS

In 1831 the German scholar K. A. Veith wrote an article entitled "Ueber ein vergessenes Werk des Geschichtschreibers Johannes Dubravius,"[1] in which he summarized the contents of a long poem, the *Theriobulia*, by the Bohemian scholar, diplomat, and bishop, Jan Dubravius. At that time the poem was so nearly forgotten that Veith could find no copy of any edition, but had to use the text reprinted in J. H. Alsted's *Compendium lexici philosophici* (Herborn, 1626). By great good fortune, however, a copy of the original edition still exists. Of all the bibliographers, only Panzer refers to it as being in the library of the Royal Society in London.[2] Since that time this copy has been acquired by Harvard University, the gift of Philip Hofer in 1941, and is now in the Houghton Library.[3] It was published by Frederick Peypus in Nuremberg on 12 March 1520. The title page of this small volume of thirty-eight unnumbered folios, bound in vellum, is adorned with a charming woodcut border attributed to Hans Springinklee. Surrounding the title, the lion-king of Bohemia, enthroned with diadem

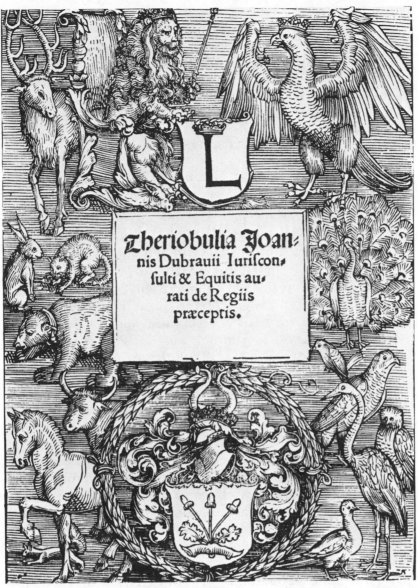

**Theriobulia Joan-
nis Dubrauii Iuriscon-
sulti & Equitis au-
rati de Regiis
præceptis.**

9.  Title page of Jan Dubravius' *Theriobulia*, Nuremberg, 1520
Houghton Library, Harvard University

and scepter, facing the crowned eagle of Moravia, is depicted with various birds and animals. An "L" crowned within a shield is centered above the title, and below it, outlined in a wreath, is a coat of arms consisting of an oak branch from which spring three acorns. The title reads: Theriobulia Johannis Dubravii Iurisconsulti et Equitis aurati de Regiis praeceptis. Another edition of the poem edited by Johannes Antoninus in Cracow in 1521 for the press of Floryan Ungler and one printed in Breslau in 1614 are recorded,[4] but I have been unable to locate a copy of either edition.

Dubravius wrote his poem on the joyful occasion of the accession of the young Louis II to the throne of Bohemia and Pannonia in a ceremony at Prague in 1517.[5] In a prose dedication, addressing Louis as *invictissime* and *clementissime*, the poet bids the new king strive to equal the singular devotion to duty of his grandfather Casimir, the incomparable integrity of his father Vladislaus, and the remarkable justice of his uncle Sigismund, king of Poland. He hopes that Louis will accept his gift happily, read it with pleasure, and wish gladly to imitate those parts which he admires. There is no indication that this was more than a private poem, and it would presumably have remained so if Dubravius' cousin, Leonard Dubravius, had 'not seen it and begged to copy it. The good bishop granted this permission on condition that he keep it for his own use. Although Leonard usually respected his cousin's wishes, in this instance he felt constrained to allow others to enjoy it; consequently, he wrote a dedication to Peter Krafft, bishop of Ratisbon, and had it published in Nuremberg in 1520.[6]

The title of the Latin poem *Theriobulia* carries the double meaning of "council of animals" and the "counsel of the animals."[7] It is written in a variety of Greek meters that had been made familiar by Horace in his Odes. It is an unusual fable written expressly for the young king at the beginning of his reign. It opens with an invitation from the new king-lion to all the birds and animals to attend a meeting. Puzzled as to the reason for the assembly, since the kingdom is at peace and there seem to be no threats from foreign or domestic foes, the creatures arrive at the palace. Immediately, with simple dignity, the lion addresses them as faithful followers and thanks them for coming. Speaking with regret of the death of his father, reminding them of his own youth and inexperience, and stating his conviction that kingly power depends more upon virtue than on royal blood, he asks them to advise him concerning the kingly virtues for which he should strive. Twenty-four quadrupeds and twenty-four birds answer the invitation and each gives the counsel that he considers most important.

If it is extraordinary by all the conventions of the traditional fable to find the lion-king sincerely seeking advice on the conduct of his personal life and the administration of his domain, it is consistent with the tenor of this whole poem. Although the animals recognize the stereotype set for them since the time of Aesop, they behave in a remarkably independent pattern. For instance, on this occasion, the normally arrogant lion is humble. He says, "Because I am a lion, do not think me so endowed with brutish feelings that I should believe my kingdom can be secure by that fact alone." Again he expresses his feeling of kingly obligation: "It is right for a king to be above all in character as he is in fortune." The wolf actually cites as a general estimate of his character the fable of the wolf who devoured an innocent lamb on the pretext that the victim was muddying the drinking water, though the poor creature was downstream from the wolf. He cautions the lion against behaving in a wolfish manner, extorting and plundering. "It is better to have a poor kingdom than a rich one that has been formed from evil gains." The fox does not show such a complete reversal of character, but she does give straightforward advice. Her warning is against unreliable administrators who will look to their own interests and against parasites who are set upon enriching themselves at the expense of the common good. The lion-king would do well to look after his affairs himself.

During the course of the meeting, as each creature emphasizes the characteristics that he thinks appropriate and requisite for a good king, there emerges a clear image of the kind of monarch they would like. First of all, he must be a Christian king, a sincere worshipper of Christ and a faithful follower of his precepts. Consistent with the Christian tradition, he should exhibit the qualities of truthfulness, justice, clemency, courage, constancy, sobriety, and patience. The king must always be honorable; in word and deed he must show himself "humanus" and magnanimous. As an administrator the king should take care to surround himself with honorable and wise counsellors. His court should be splendid and magnificent, affording generous hospitality and noble entertainment particularly to representatives of other states. By vigilance and preparedness he should keep his country strong against external enemies and free from internal lawlessness and crime. His goal should always be peace.

These abstract qualifications for the ideal ruler represent the sum total of the positive injunctions of the various creatures, but the individual admonitions are expressed in specific terms, often in a colorful style. So, for example, the leopard begins his advice on the need for learning by declaring, on the authority of Homer, that Calliope, the chief of the Muses, is the companion of kings, and reminds the lion that Plato asks that kings be educated and love those who are learned. Bidding the king to discover his own nature, the flamingo urges him never to violate his natural integrity. The ox, disclaiming talent and wisdom, suggests the homely advice that the king walk with slow and deliberate step, yet always in a firm and unwavering course. The monkey advocates a touch of humor to leaven the usual gravity of the monarch, but always in good taste and consistent with the dignity and majesty of the position. The donkey, out of his long experience of burden-bearing, urges the king to endure the great burdens of state with fortitude and equanimity. With phrases reminiscent of Tibullus, the deer enumerates and extols the blessings of peace, recommending the constant pursuit of harmony and concord. To reinforce the sentiments of the deer, the eagle reminds the lion that of the two ways of settling differences between peoples, that is, war and lawful arbitration, violence is the way of beasts, while a peaceful resolution of conflicting interests is more appropriate for men. With greater acumen than he is generally credited with, the camel reminds the lion of two precepts of Plato: to bend all of his efforts to the common good and to think of the state as an organic whole, never to cater to one part to the neglect of another. Recommending compassion for the poor, the falcon reminds the lion that he should always consider himself the father of his people.

Not every animal is sufficiently tactful to phrase his advice in the form of constructive suggestions: many, indeed, choose to concentrate upon qualities and situations to be avoided. Curiously enough, often the most timorous, mild creatures are most vehement in their admonitions. The dove, for example, in strong terms, warns against giving way to anger. Rage, one step removed from frenzy, unable to control itself, forgetful of honor, foe to reason, is bound to result in ruin. A hundred tongues, a hundred throats, and a voice of iron could not describe the myriad evils resultant from anger in a king. After endorsing the strictures of the dove, the lamb warns against intemperate speech, condemning particularly several proverbial sayings associated with tyrants, such as the one made famous by Euripides' Hippolytus, "Though I have sworn with my tongue, yet my mind never committed itself." In line with these two is the injunction of the ibis that the king should refrain from saying anything of which he might later be ashamed. Further, Caesar's house must be free even of the suspicion of wrong. Many of the creatures warn against personal failings, such as sensuality, love of luxury, arrogance, pride, indolence, deceitfulness, perfidy, avarice, sloth, drunkenness, and licentiousness. Only a few point out pitfalls to be avoided in governing the state. Do not, they warn, demoralize the soldiers by distributing largess; do not allow the state to be divided by heretical groups lest it perish; do not plunder and destroy the enemy, once he has been conquered; do not be influenced by evil advisers.

The animals and birds to a large extent abandon the fiction of the lion-king and speak in human terms. Examples to illustrate some quality which they wish to emphasize are often taken from Greek literature or Greek and Roman history. The goose, for example, points out that the ideal for a king and his people is best demonstrated in the picture that Homer paints of the highly cultured king Alcinous and his civilized people, the Phaeaceans. Plato is recommended for his discussion of the role of the king with respect to ensuring the highest welfare of the people. As models to emulate, one or another of the creatures names the Roman heroes: Cato, Brutus, Camillus, Aemilius Paulus, and Horatius Cocles, for their devotion to duty and their constancy and endurance. Again, as worthy examples, they cite Scipio for his memorable insistence upon the sacred rights of legates, Augustus for his urbanity and culture, and Trajan, Hadrian, and Alexander Severus for their magnificence and splendor in court life and in imperial buildings. Many more of the ancients serve as exponents of behavior to be avoided. Among them, Agamemnon is held up as an example of failure in leadership through  indecision; Tarquinius Superbus and Sulla demonstrate the folly of cruelty and arrogance; Alexander the Great exemplifies intemperance in every form; the Roman emperors Caligula, Nero, and Commodus exhibit depraved conduct not only unworthy of a monarch but most ruinous to a state.

Several of the former rulers of Bohemia are cited to illustrate the animals' ideas. Charles IV, king of Bohemia from 1346 to 1378, who made Prague a beautiful city resplendent with noble public buildings and majestic churches and founded the great university, is recalled as an illustrious example of the creator of a magnificent capitol and a splendid court. On the other hand, the brilliant promise of Charles's son, Wenceslaus IV of Germany and king of Bohemia from 1378 to 1419, a promise that failed to materialize because of vacillation and lack of adequate leadership, is an illustration of the disastrous results of intemperance. Wenceslaus' half-brother, Sigismund of Poland, whom Wenceslaus placed upon the throne of Hungary and who succeeded him as king of Bohemia (1436-1437), is lauded because he made his palace a showplace of elegance and provided lavish hospitality suitable to his position. Although he was king of Bohemia for only two years (1469-1471), the brilliant Matthias Corvinus of Hungary is thrice cited not solely for his wealth, culture, and glittering court, but more for his humility and concern for even the least of his subjects. Matthias, who has the reputation of being one of the greatest monarchs who ever reigned, yielded the throne of Bohemia to Vladislaus (1471-1516), the father of young Louis, who later succeeded him as king of Hungary also. The generous entertainment provided by Vladislaus is noted with favorable comment, for ambassadors and visiting royalty were always laden with precious gifts and given safe conduct through Bohemia and Pannonia in accord with the sacred rights of envoys. Louis himself, Ludovicus II, king of Hungary and Bohemia (1517-1526), though only a boy at the time, is praised for his bravery in war against the Turks.

Dubravius' long poem is interrupted at mid-point after twenty-two of the creatures have spoken. Then the lion-king dismisses the assembly. In seemly manner the participants retire to the royal palace where a splendid banquet has been prepared. In a scene recalling the feast of the gods at the end of the first book of the *Iliad*, the king, his nobles, and all the subjects sit down before well-laden tables served by one hundred animals and one hundred birds. After dinner the king drinks a toast to the queen eagle, then all drink freely from golden goblets while the nightingale plays upon the lyre. Finally, sleep, invited by the sweet strains of the harp, comes and stands at the door. The king arises and goes to his chamber and all the guests go to their repose.

The second book opens with a pleasant picture of the dawning of the new day as the birds leave their nests and the animals come from their dens in the forest or their marshy glades. The lion-king again convenes the assembly and twenty-six other creatures speak their views. At the end, fourteen more bid the bison serve as their spokesman. He responds with eloquent rhetoric in a series of conditional clauses in which he delineates the qualifications he considers essential in a king, then declaring, "Such a man we truly call a Christian king." Without further comment the king rises from his ivory throne and the animals escort him into the palace.

The antecedents for Dubravius' poem were, first, the fables attributed to Aesop, in all their varying adaptations from Avianus through Gualterus Anglicus, then the related medieval beast epic, from Isengrimus of Master Nisardus of Ghent, through uncounted versions of Reynard the Fox tales, particularly in the Netherlands, Germany, and France. Curiously enough, the core of these tales is the story of the sick lion and the council of animals. Here one finds the chief actors cast in persisting roles: the arrogant lion, the vicious wolf, and the crafty, heartless fox. The *Physiologus*, too, and its transformation in various medieval bestiaries, furnished knowledge of the same animals and gave information on many more. Although Dubravius knew many of these earlier works, his immediate and specific source is revealed in his dedication. Here he tells Louis that, most happily, at precisely the right moment, he came upon an old animal fable in the vernacular which told of a meeting of animals to counsel their new king. This book, also written in poetry, is the Czech *Nová Rada* of Smil Fláška of Pardupitz, the secretary of state of Bohemia from 1396 to 1403.[8] Composed about 1394 in the reign of Wenceslaus IV,[9] it was published several times in the sixteenth century and recently (1940) a very charming adaptation in modern Czech by František Vrba was published in Prague. The title *New Counsels* indicates that it, too, was based upon an older account.[10] In Fláška's Czech poem most of the birds and animals are the same ones who speak in Dubravius' work; they are all real creatures, with the exception of the griffin and the unicorn who do not appear in the *Theriobulia*.[11] The assembly takes the form of a parliament where the animals debate, taking opposite sides in their advice, while the Latin-speaking animals of Dubravius always present their advice from the point of view of loyalty to the king. Fláška's poem is an allegory, full of symbolism like the bestiaries, quite medieval in flavor, reminiscent of Chaucer's *Parliament of Fowls,* and there is the humor one associates with medieval tales. It is the poetry of the common Bohemian people, the laymen who are concerned with the reformation of abuses in the Church, in contrast to the poetry of Dubravius where the animals speak from the side of the established Church, and, in fact, warn against the Protestant sects as heretical. Although the Czech poem reveals no interest in landscape and background, it has some dramatic episodes, while the *Theriobulia* has some fine passages describing natural scenery, but it is not theatrical. The animals in the first poem are natural and simple; in the second they are creatures of wit and wide learning. Dubravius' transformation of a lively animal allegory into a learned poem was a most appropriate gift to the precocious youth, Louis, who was studious, gentle and kind by nature, yet eager to prove himself a brave and strong king.

The author of the *Theriobulia,* Jan Dubravius (Johannes Dubravius, Jan Dubraw), achieved distinction as a Churchman, historian, and diplomat, but it is his role as a humanist that particularly concerns us. Born in Pilsen in 1486, he was originally named Johannes Skala. After he had gone through the local schools, he was sent to Vienna to study because the University of Prague at that time was under the control of the heretical Utraquist sect. In Vienna, under the guidance of the brilliant German humanist, Conrad Celtis, he became versed in rhetoric and Classical literature. He then studied in several universities in Italy until he earned the degree of Doctor of Ecclesiastical Law at Padua. In 1511 he returned to Bohemia to become the secretary of the scholar Stanislaus Thurzo, Bishop of Olmütz, who was friend to many of the northern humanists, including Erasmus. Serving in a number of ecclesiastical posts, he had opportunities to become acquainted with many scholars, among whom he counted the German humanist, Caspar Ursinus Velius, his life-long friend. Because of his eloquence and legal skill, he was entrusted with diplomatic missions in various countries. So, for example, he was sent to the court of Francesco

Sforza of Milan to arrange the marriage of King Sigismund and the Duke's daughter. Shortly after Louis was crowned King of Bohemia by Bishop Thurzo, he was elevated to the knighthood and became *eques auratus*. At the same time he was given the arms of Doubravka and Hradisch with the right thereafter to be called Dubravius. For his services in trying to effect an end to the Turkish threats to Hungary, he was granted the castle and town of Bretzstaw. After the battle of Mohács (1526), Dubravius himself led a regiment against the Turks. In 1541, at the death of Bishop Thurzo, he was elected Bishop of Olmütz. The remaining years of his life were occupied by endless political problems in Bohemia, Hungary, Moravia, and Poland, and by the most agonizing troubles within the Church, not only with the menace of the Turks but with the Protestant sects that were dividing the country by civil war.

In spite of his official duties, Dubravius found time to write an impressive number of works. They are: *Commentary on Martianus Capella, Oration to King Sigismund against the Turks, Oration on the Marriage of Sigismund, Letter on the Liturgy,* and *Commentary on Psalm V.* More extensive in scope are his two best-known books: a comprehensive *History of Bohemia,* and a *Treatise on Fishponds and Fish,* which was translated into English in 1599, and was widely read in England.[12]

In the *Theriobulia* Dubravius shows himself a humanist both in the style of his poetry and in the content. The very fact that the animals speak Latin, although they had been talking in French, German, and Czech for several hundred years, makes the work a scholar's poem. Besides numerous ancient proverbs and the fables, the animals know Greek mythology and ancient history. They have read the works of many of the Roman and several of the Greek writers as one sees from frequent references. They quote Homer, Plato, Plautus, Cicero, Ovid, Seneca, Suetonius, and Ausonius. Much more often, however, they provide the reader the pleasure of recognition as they reproduce scenes, lines, or phrases from Classical literature in alien contexts.[13]

In content, too, the *Theriobulia* is a product of the humanistic attitude toward society. Heir to a long series of medieval
*Speculum principis* treatises, the Renaissance literature
about the ideal prince retains most of the old moral teachings,
but it is less stereotyped, more imaginative, and more
liberal, placing more emphasis upon education and human
worth. In Italy the new trend begins with Petrarch who, in
a letter often entitled *De principis officio,* written in 1350,
gives *Dogmata seu praecepta* to insure the welfare of both
prince and state. The virtues to be cultivated, the vices to be
avoided, the qualities of statesmanship to be striven for, and
the honor of the state are topics that Petrarch reviews for
Niccolò Acciaiuoli, seneschal to the King of Sicily.[11] A century later Giovanni Pontano, secretary to Ferdinand I of
Naples and chief literary figure of the Neapolitan Academy,
dedicated his *Liber de principe* to Alfonso of Calabria.
Written informally, in the guise of a letter, it repeats all the
kingly virtues and recalls the various pitfalls waiting for
the unwary ruler, but it chiefly stresses the spirit of human
dignity and *humanitas,* as it advocates the pursuit of learning.
These two works seem close to the spirit of Dubravius' words
of counsel to the young King Louis in his animal fable which,
in reality, is a mirror for the prince.

It is an interesting phenomenon that a number of famous
books on the education of the prince and the ideal state
appeared just about the time that Dubravius wrote his work:
Machiavelli's *Il Principe* written in 1513, Castiglione's *Il
Cortegiano* in 1514, More's *Utopia* in 1516, and Erasmus'
*Institutio principis Christiani* in 1516. Only the last can
well be compared to the *Theriobulia,* for Machiavelli's
prince is too disillusioned, Castiglione's court life is more
worldly than the pleasant society of the Phaeaceans recommended by Dubravius, and More's state is too largely concerned with political and economic theory. Although Erasmus'
*The Education of the Christian Prince* was written for Prince
Charles (later Charles V), grandson of the Emperor Maximilian, who was living in circumstances as different as
possible from Bohemia's Louis, and Erasmus was writing

a systematic treatise on the proper education for the head of state, yet the atmosphere that pervades the book and many of the subjects discussed seem close to Dubravius' work. If one were to single out three precepts for the prince that Erasmus seems to stress more than others, they would be: Be a sincere Christian: Show human kindness and understanding under all circumstances: Above all, cherish peace. Dubravius' animals, as we have seen, give similar advice to their lion-king. For us, too, these precepts elicit a sympathetic response as the eagle bids the lion worship God with a pure heart and singleness of mind, as the falcon recommends the qualities of gentleness, mercy, and kindness that make an individual truly *humanus*, as the deer pleads for the blessings of peace, and as the elephant says confidently that under a just king peace and concord will surely prevail.

*Part V*

**Early Printed Books**

# MANUSCRIPTS COPIED

# FROM PRINTED BOOKS

"The invention of the press came at a time exactly suitable for its advent."[1] Although the economic factors of the availability of an abundant supply of paper and an increasing literate population were the chief reasons for this situation, contributory to it was an important human factor: both the scribes and the authors were ready for the printed book. Witness to this are the many colophons penned by weary copyists. Of these, one of the most restrained, yet most effective, is a single hexameter line, in heavy spondees, that occurs in a twelfth-century manuscript from the Abbey of St. Victor (Paris, lat. 14954, f. 92$^r$). At the end of a dull commentary on Martianus Capella the scribe wrote, "Now at last, little quill, you have finished your very long task."[2] If the scribes complained of their tedious work, the authors, too, were impatient, chiefly with the imperfect workmanship of the scribes. Petrarch, for instance, frequently speaks with bitterness of the indolence and ignorance of scribes that have caused "an incredible loss to scholarship, as books of a difficult nature have ceased to be intelligible, and, completely

Ἀρτι παὶ γρου·

Οὖρσ ὀλ⳥ανδροιο δια πλοοσ· οὖρς ὁ πόντ⳥ου·
Πορθμὸς, ὁ μἠ μούνῳ τῷ Φιλέ⳥ντι βαρύς·
Ταῦθἦρούς τα πάροιθε πο⳥Γαύλια· ρῦ⳥ρ ρὸ πύ⳥ρ⳥ρου
Λεί ψανον· ὁ προδότης ὦ δἔ⳥πέ⳥λιἀ⳥ρ λύχνος·
Κοινὸς δἀ⳥μφοτέρους ὁ Δ⳥ἔ⳥χ⳥ τάφος, εἰ⳥σέτι καὶ νῦ⳥
Κείνῳ το⳥̑ φθονε⳥ρ⳥ὼ μεμφομἱ⳥ψουσ ανέ μῳ·

10. Copy of two woodcuts from Aldus' *Opusculum de*
*Herone et Leandro*

Antipatri.

Hic est Leandri tranatus. hoc est ponti
  Fretum non soli amanti graue.
Hæc Herûs antiquæ domicilia· hæ turris
  Reliquiæ· proditrix hic pendebat lucerna.
·Cõmunéq; ambos hoc habet sepulchrum, nũc quoq;
  De illo inuido conquerentes uento.

Clamabat tumidis audax Leander ĩ undis.
  Parcite dũ propo. mergite dũ redeo.

neglected by everybody, have perished in the end."[3] One
also recalls Chaucer's harsh words to his own scrivener:

> Adam scriveyn, if ever thee befalle
> Boece or Troylus for to wryten newe,
> Under thy long lokkes thou most have the scalle,
> But after my makyng thou wryte more trewe;
> So ofte a-daye I mot thy werk renewe,
> It to correcte and eek to rubbe and scrape;
> And all is through thy negligence and rape.[4]

Even after the introduction of a more economical and faster
method of copying manuscripts, the so-called "pecia" system
used largely in such university centers as Bologna and Paris
for the production of textbooks, whereby the whole text
was divided into many sections and distributed to a number
of copyists at the same time,[5] there was still dissatisfaction,
presumably on both sides. At least one of the scribes of such
a manuscript has registered his feelings in a note on a Yale
manuscript (MS 207)[6] of Thomas Aquinas' Commentary on
the third book of the "Sentences" of Peter Lombard, a
thirteenth-century manuscript from the Cistercian monastery of Royaumont in the diocese of Senlis. At the foot of the
second column of folio 47[r] the scribe had, apparently, written
five lines beyond the text of the first column. Then it would
seem that the bookseller caught the irregularity and instructed
the scribe to erase the additional lines. This meant that
there had to be an adjustment on the following page. It looks
as if consequently the first eleven lines had been erased to
accommodate the extra material that was then crowded into
the space, and even at that the last fifteen words had to be
written in the margin. The scribe, no doubt chagrined by the
unfortunate appearance of the two pages, added at the bottom
of the page (which he may have thought would be cut off in
the binding), "Confound the stationer who has caused me to
disfigure the book of some honest man."[7]

Since, then, conditions were propitious for the change from
the hand-written book to the machine-printed book, and

particularly since the conversion was a gradual, slow, and uneven process, it would seem that a minimum of difficulty and dislocation was experienced. Of course for decades after the first printed books became available, many scribes continued to copy manuscripts in their accustomed way in scriptoria all over Europe.[8] When the change to printing did come, whether early or late, naturally manuscripts had to serve as printers' copy. There is an interesting manuscript in Yale collection (MS 321) that was used as copy for the printing of the first edition of the Italian translation of Poggio-Bracciolini's *Historia Florentina* made by his son Jacopo. The manuscript, written in 1475, is a large paper codex of 140 folios, in a fine humanistic script, with two decorative initials and others painted in blue. In using the manuscript, the printer indicated with a bracket in black ink in the text the beginning of each printed page, and added a further guide mark in the margin. In the printed book (Yale Zi. +4243) the pages coincide exactly with the indications in the manuscript.[9] So slavish is the copy that space was left for the initials that were never added in the printed text. Some corrections in the hand-written text, apparently made by the printer, for example, the regular change from *e* to *&* and the verb *avere* to *havere*, are followed in the printed text. In spite of having been used in the printer's shop, where some manuscripts apparently had to be discarded, the original manuscript is still a beautiful book.

The reverse of this normal process of copying manuscripts to make printed editions, that is, copying incunabula to make hand-written books,[10] is demonstrated by a number of interesting books in the Beinecke Library. The first is a manuscript copy of Cicero's *Pro Marcello* (Zi. +2073) written in Germany about 1500. It was copied, on paper, in a rather careless cursive hand, with wide spaces left between lines for notes, from a Leipzig edition printed by Konrad Kachelofen about 1492.[11] The short text of ten folios is bound into a large volume with four texts, printed between 1486 and 1495,[12] presumably to serve as a textbook for a Leipzig professor. The only plausible explanation for the inclusion of the *Pro Marcello* in manuscript is that the compiler was unable to obtain a printed text.

A second example of a manuscript copy of a printed text occurs in a book containing a collection of five incunables printed between 1475 and 1480 (Zi 6937.6). The hand-written treatise consists of three folios written in a gothic script, and the text is a poem of Pope Pius II (Aeneas Sylvius Piccolomini) entitled *Carmen Sapphicum,* a hymn in Sapphic verse on the Passion, dedicated to Frederick III. Fortunately the copyist revealed his source when he added the colophon of the printed edition: Impressum est in Augusta per Gintherum Zainer de Reutlingenn. Curiously enough, no edition by Gunther Zainer of Augsburg has yet been found. The poem is printed (pp. 963-964) with the collected works of Pius II published in Basel in 1571. Its presence with the prose incunables[13] can only be attributed to the personal choice of the editor.

Another example of this phenomenon is a small volume (MS 451) of fourteen folios bound in black morocco, containing three orations by prominent humanists, all written in the same small careful, cursive hand. The first, the *Oratio in conventu Ratisponensi ad exhortandos principes Germanorum contra Turcos anno 1471 habita,* was delivered by Johannes Antonius Campanus (Giovanni Antonio Campano), bishop of Teramo. The printed book from which it was copied was the first edition printed by Stephan Plannck about 1487 (Yale Zi. 3732). Both manuscript and printed edition have two mistakes in the title which were corrected in the second edition (ca. 1488/1490) *Ratispo* for *Ratisponensi* and *exhortandas* for *exhortandos.* The second speech, *Oratio pronunciata in senatu Venetiarum,* is the work of Johannes de Margarit, bishop of Gerona, Spain, a versatile scholar noted for his brilliance as an orator. It includes the printer's colophon: Hanc orationem impressit Georgius theotonicus ex ordinatione magnifici domini Johannis Philippi de lignamine militis messanensis. The book from which it was taken was printed in Rome by Georgius Teutonicus, 24 July 1481, for Johannes Philippus de Lignamine.

The third, the *Oratio in funere Leonardi de Robore*, was delivered by Franciscus de Toleto, bishop of Coria, better known as François Busleiden, archbishop of Besancon. The printed text from which it was taken is found in a small volume (Yale Zi. 3737) printed in Rome by Stephan Plannck between 1481 and 1487. The copy is so close that here the scribe even left a space for the first initial which was never put in, exactly following the printed work. There is no indication of provenance in the manuscript, but it is safe to conjecture that it was made for some scholar who wished to have combined in one book these notable examples of various types of contemporary oratory.

Quite different is the case of another manuscript (MS 508) recently acquired by Yale, the gift of the Yale Library Associates. It is a volume written in an Icelandic hand containing the Icelandic text of the *Annals of Iceland* extending from 636 to 1394 and covering events in Scandinavia, Iceland, and Greenland. It is a paper book, written in Iceland about 1600. Somewhat later it seems to have been rebound and at that time two quires of different paper were added at the beginning. They were subsequently (ca. 1700) filled with a hand-written copy of the *Foedus Edouardi et Guthruni* and a large part of the *Leges Edouardi regis*. These two early documents relating to English history, the Treaty between Edward the Elder and Guthrun II, King of the Danes in East Anglia (905-906), and the Laws of Edward the Confessor (died 1066), were copied from a printed book that is reputed to be the first book in Anglo-Saxon printed in England. It is the *APXAINOMIA sive de priscis legibus libri*, edited by William Lambarde and first printed in London in 1568 (Yale Ib 22. t568). The printed book has the Anglo-Saxon text on the left-hand page and the Latin translation on the right. The copyist took only the Latin text,[14] but he followed this so exactly that he has reproduced all the printed marginal comments and indicated them with the same markings.

Among the Yale books, by far the most striking example of a manuscript copied from a printed book is that of a handsome facsimile of one of the rare early Aldine books (now MS 534). This fine volume, meticulously written on superb vellum and bound by Bozérian Jeune in dark blue morocco with the Aldine anchor in gilt on both covers,[15] was probably made about 1800 for some wealthy book collector who specialized in Aldines and was unable to obtain an original copy of this work. Such a person was Sir John Thorold[16] who bought a great many books in Paris and assembled an impressive group of incunabula in his library at Syston Park. His bookplate, along with the monogram book-label of his son, Sir John Hayford Thorold, who was also a great collector of Aldines, occurs inside the front cover of the Yale book. When the Syston Park library was sold, the noted American bibliophile, William Loring Andrews, purchased it and presented it to Yale in 1894.

The text of the Aldine book, the romantic and tragic poem of *Hero and Leander* by Musaeus, is of more than usual interest.[17] The original Musaeus was a completely legendary poet associated with Orpheus. The author of the poem was another Musaeus who lived, probably in Alexandria, in the fifth century of our era. Renaissance scholars, however, and among them the keen Julius Caesar Scaliger,[18] identified the later poet with the pre-Homeric singer and expressed the greatest admiration for his work which they considered the oldest poem in existence. Besides being a graceful poem, it relates a touching tale that appealed to countless later writers from Marlowe to Schiller, Byron, and Keats. Another reason for its popularity may be that, as it is written in a straightforward style in simple language, the humanists, with their scanty Greek, could understand and enjoy it. It was not, therefore, by pure chance, that the poem was printed very early in five countries: by Lorenzo di Alopa (Zi. 6411) in Florence about 1494; by Aldus Manutius (Zi. 5545) in Venice about 1494; by Egidius Gourmontius (Gfm83. b515) in Paris about 1515; by Arnaldo Guillen de Brocar in Alcalá in 1514; by Eucharius Cervicornus in Cologne in 1517; and by Henri Estienne in Geneva in 1566.

Musaeus' *Opusculum de Herone et Leandro* is generally considered to be the second book ever published by Aldus

Manutius, and although no date is given in the book, it must have been printed about 1494-1495. There are at Yale three Aldine editions of the book. The first (Zi. 5545, copy 1), edited by the great Cretan scholar, Marcus Musurus, has the Greek text with the Latin translation, probably also by Musurus, interleaved. Preceding the text there is a Greek preface by Aldus in which he calls Musaeus the oldest of the poets,[19] and two epigrams of Musurus in both languages. In the center of the book there are two woodcuts on facing pages: one representing Hero on the tower waiting for Leander who is swimming across the Hellespont, and the second showing Hero leaping from the window of her tower at the foot of which lies the lifeless body of her lover drowned by the stormy seas.[20] There is a short epigram of Antipater (*Greek Anthology* VII.666) in Greek and Latin above the woodcuts. The Greek type font of a cursive style is thought to have been designed by Musurus. The title page must have been added when the book had been completed, for on the verso the editor has noted two *errata*. Since two lines were omitted from the text, he gives the exact location and quotes the two lines in both languages. There follows, also in both languages, a two-line epitaph for Musaeus. At the end of the page there is a surprising note, for the editor says that since the Greek lexicographer Suidas[21] gives four writers named Musaeus, there is a question concerning the identity of the author of the poem. Although in some copies of this first edition of the book a few typographical errors were indicated, probably by the editor,[22] none of these appears in this copy.

The second Yale copy (Zi.5545, copy 2) has the Greek text only, including the Greek poems of Musurus, identical with the first, but the woodcuts are lacking. Yet the title page of the first, including the *errata* and the epitaph in both languages, is used in this volume.[23] Both books are considered the *editio princeps*, and it has been suggested that Aldus was thus prepared to sell the poem in Greek alone or with the translation.[24] The third volume (Gfm83.b517), printed in 1517 after Aldus' death, is quite different; the

Greek and the Roman type are smaller and the woodcuts are correspondingly reduced in size and show some variations from the earlier ones. The Greek and Latin versions occur on facing pages. A number of editor's corrections to the earlier text, as well as the two lines omitted in the first, appear in the correct forms in this book. The volume includes three short works attributed to Orpheus.

The facsimile copy is like the *editio princeps* in every respect except that the entire Latin text follows the Greek, rather than being interleaved, and the woodcuts occur after the Greek and preceding the Latin text. The signature letters for the Greek: $\alpha$ i, $\alpha$ ii, $\alpha$ iii, $\alpha$ iiii, $\alpha$ iiiii, and even the faulty ones for the Latin: *b, c, b*iiii, v, *b*vi, are the same. The printer's arabesques at the head of several pages are reproduced with amazing exactitude; the copies of the woodcuts mimic the originals except in very minor details. Even the Greek colophon giving the place of printing and the name of the printer is copied faithfully. A few typographical errors, *e.g. invidiam* for *iniuriam* (signature *b*, line 17) and *lirora* for *litora* (folio 19$^r$, line 19) appear just as they are in the printed book. Only a rare scribal error, such as *quaerendam* for *quaerendum* at the end of the verso of the title page, betrays the fallability of the copyist. So far as he was able, however, the scribe produced an identical replica of the incunable. A palaeographer, looking at the original side by side with the beautiful facsimile, might be pardoned for passing such biased judgment as: *matre pulchra, filia pulchrior.*

# An Unusual Educational Device
## of Aldus Manutius

Aldus Pius Manutius' brilliant reputation as a printer has tended to obscure the fact that he was by temperament and through choice primarily and consistently throughout his life a dedicated teacher.

By a curious irony the circumstances that influenced Aldus to direct his life toward teaching were the very ones that must have driven many another away from scholarship entirely. Aldus says[1] that as a boy in Rome he had an inept instructor who compelled the pupils to memorize all of Alexandre de Villedieu's *Doctrinale,* a Latin grammar of 26,000 lines in rhymed hexameter. The dullness and pedantry of the book, written in 1199 and used almost exclusively for three hundred years, made vivid to Aldus the pressing need for a suitable Latin grammar since that was the foundation for all education.

As a teacher himself for twenty years, Aldus had ample opportunity for experimenting with methods of presenting Latin grammar, particularly during the years (1483-90) when he served as tutor to the two nephews of Pico della Mirandola, the young princes of the house of Carpi. In a letter to the learned mother of the boys, Catharine Pio, on the subject of the education of her sons, he reveals his affection for the children and his attitude toward education. He says[2] that he has composed a Latin grammar adapted to the needs of young pupils, and two small treatises, one on the accents and pronunciation of Latin and one on writing poetry. In order to compliment the boys on their progress and to encourage their efforts, he has also written for Prince Alberto a Panegyric of the Muses, a poem in which each of the Muses sings in honor of the boy's accomplishments;[3] for his brother Leonello, he has written a poem which contains simple precepts for good conduct.[4] Both compositions are accompanied by brief Greek quotations. He explains to the mother that a child should, as early as possible, learn Latin and Greek simultaneously. He stresses the necessity for proficiency in both languages for correct and forceful speech. Chiefly, however, he emphasizes the need for moral training as he insists that the children be taught to love virtue.[5]

When Aldus left the classroom for what he considered the wider arena of education for a larger circle of scholars whom he could best serve by editing and printing texts, he composed a kind of *Religio magistri*. In the epilogue to his *Institutionum grammaticarum libri quatuor*, an enlargment of the book he wrote for the Carpi princes, he states,[6] "I have vowed to devote my whole life to service to my fellow men. God is my witness that I desire nothing more than to benefit men . . . and to this end I shall direct my every effort. Though I might live a quiet and peaceful life, I have chosen one that is full of activity and difficulties. Man was not born for pleasures unworthy of a good and enlightened soul, but for performing his duty and for constantly doing what is worthy of him."

This Latin grammar, printed in 1501[7] and in thirteen later editions, demonstrates most effectively Aldus' teaching methods. First of all, he knows that he must indoctrinate the teachers who will use the book, so he addresses a long preface to them. Reminding them of their grave responsibility for directing and shaping the very lives of their pupils, he charges them to lead virtuous lives themselves and to develop sound moral characters in their pupils while they are teaching the fundamentals of language and speech. After a long harangue, he concludes, "I should rather have the pupils know no letters at all, provided they are good and honorable, than that they should know everything, but have no moral standards."[8] More briefly he instructs the teachers in procedure. He urges them to require the pupils to memorize only the basic rules of grammar; he particularly advises against forcing them to learn long passages, a practice that may cause them to hate both the study and the school. Only when the boys have acquired a certain competency so that they can enjoy it, should they be introduced to select passages of Cicero and Virgil.

As Aldus always assumes that the pupils are eager to learn, both at the beginning and at the end of his Latin grammar he provides material which any educated person should have among his mental furnishings. Before he begins the grammar, he gives the Latin text of the Lord's Prayer, the Salutation to the Virgin (both of these also in Greek), the Apostles' Creed, the Ten Commandments, the beginning of the Gospel of St. John, a morning and an evening prayer, four blessings at meals, and the Introit of the Mass, all of which he says a Christian child should know.

Very gently Aldus introduces the pupil to the intricacies of Latin grammar by presenting the alphabet, then he separates the consonants from the vowels and diphthongs, and finally gives all the syllables that can be formed from the various combinations of consonants with vowels. This brief prelude is followed by a charming elegiac poem addressed to the potential student whom he calls "parvus Iulus," promising that he will be led, not over steep cliffs nor through trackless ways, but by peaceful slopes and flowery meadows to the abode of the Muses. The long exposition of grammar is divided into four books dealing with (1) the parts of grammar, the noun and pronoun and their inflection, (2) the verb and its inflection, the adverb, (3) the grammatical constructions, figures of speech, (4) metrics. Aldus' method is a modified catechetical one, as he presents his topics in the form of questions and answers, always with examples from the Roman writers. Since, in general, it is more of a compendium than a teaching manual, and of course it is all in Latin,[9] it places a heavy responsibility upon the teacher for elucidating and illustrating the various subjects. Even though it is of necessity an objective text, yet one feels the personality of the author in his presentation, particularly in his examples. In the first part of the grammar he gives simple illustrations, always from the ancient writers, but as he reaches the more complicated constructions he assumes that his pupil has progressed so he includes longer passages and mentions less well-known writers, sometimes giving references to literary characters. Toward the end he even includes a few contemporary references such as one to Ferdinand and Isabella of Spain.[10] Aldus' enthusiasm for poetry and the varied meters used in Latin and Greek carries him beyond what his grammar promised or indeed required, as he provides the scansion for the most complicated meters and gives long passages in them. At the end he confesses that he has given more than the table of contents indicated.[11]

Though he has said the last word on Latin grammar, Aldus' zeal for imparting knowledge continues unabated. To satisfy the assumed eagerness of the pupils for still more learning, he then adds as an Appendix a section on Greek which he thinks they can easily teach themselves. First there is the alphabet printed with the Latin equivalents above, then a full discussion of the vowels and diphthongs, followed by a treatment of the consonants and the changes some undergo under special circumstances, then an explanation of the transliteration into Latin. There is also a brief section on common abbreviations in Greek. Finally, certain texts, always written with the Latin above, are given: The Lord's Prayer, the two Salutations to the Virgin, the Apostles' Creed, the first fourteen verses of the Gospel of St. John, the Golden Verses of Pythagoras, and Phocylides' Poem on the Good Life. For the student who has persevered to the end, there is a bonus in the form of a short introduction to the Hebrew language. Aldus explains that one cannot properly understand Holy Scripture without a knowledge of Hebrew, and so he prints the Hebrew alphabet and important combinations of letters, with the Latin written above, followed by the Lord's Prayer, the most commonly used Hebrew names, and the inscription written above the Cross in Hebrew, Greek, and Latin. There is the further promise that, *Deo volente*, Aldus will prepare a Hebrew grammar, dictionary, and texts of the sacred books if this introduction is well received.

Just about the time that Aldus printed his Latin grammar, he also published the Greek grammar of his friend, Constantine Lascaris, the distinguished Byzantine scholar. Aldus' first edition of this *Erotemata*, the first book he ever printed that can be dated, appeared in 1494-95, in response, he tells us, to an increasing demand from students because no Greek grammar was available to them. It is printed with a Latin translation[12] on alternate pages in regular quaternions.[13] Following the text, he presents the same introduction to Greek including the same short texts, though without the introduction to Hebrew, that he printed later in his Latin grammar. It is the 1501-1502 edition,[14] however, that is of special interest because it exhibits what surely must be considered a unique educational device. In this volume Lascaris' grammar with Aldus' translation is followed by exactly the same supplementary introduction to Greek with the same texts and the same brief introduction to Hebrew that he used in the Latin grammar. The unusual feature of the book is that it was prepared to be of use to three groups of readers: those who knew some Greek and would not need the help of the Latin, those who would not know any Greek and so would be frightened away if they did not have a parallel Latin translation, and those who may already have had access to the Greek and wished only the Latin translation.[15]

At the end of the volume Aldus has printed directions to the binder on the order of the quires if the Greek text is to be printed alone, if the Latin text is to be printed alone, and if the Latin is to be interleaved with the Greek. This last arrangement, which apparently was most in demand, required some ingenuity in the planning to insure parallel texts throughout. In theory the binder would use a quaternion of eight double folios each placed inside the earlier folio in this way: $\alpha1$, a1, $\beta2$, b2, $\gamma3$, c3, $\delta4$, d4, making a gathering of sixteen folios, with the Greek text on the first and last pages. The next quaternion would begin and end with the Latin text, and so on. Unfortunately, however, such an arrangement would mean that the two center leaves of the first quaternion would consist of two Latin, and of the second, two Greek pages facing. Aldus solved this problem and explains to his readers how he did it. He says that he could have left the two center pages blank but that would be wasteful of paper.[16] Necessity provided this opportunity for an educational advantage. On these two facing pages in the center of each quire he printed an entirely unrelated text, in both Greek and Latin facing each other. The text he selected was the *Tabula* attributed to Cebes, a moral tale that Aldus says will be beneficial to all, particularly to young students. Certainly it would arouse the curiosity of the reader as he came upon it in the first place and then discovered at the foot of the page the direction: "Look for the continuation of this in the center of the next quaternion." Aldus' own recommendation of this fine little proto-*Pilgrim's Progress* is this: "The *Tablet* of Cebes in Greek and in Latin, a useful and moral work in which the condition of human life is ingeniously set forth. The path toward virtue is shown to be narrow, steep and full of difficulties, and he who wishes to attain it must first exercise self-control and hold firm to his purpose, but finally when he has reached it, he will enjoy everlasting happiness. On the contrary, the path to vice is wide and flat and full of pleasures, but eventually leads to eternal wretchedness and misery."

The Cebes text, a great favorite with the scholars of the fifteeenth and sixteenth centuries, was eminently suitable for Aldus' purpose.[17] The Greek is easy, the vocabulary simple, and the narrative perfectly straightforward. One

could imagine that it would come as an agreeable interlude
to a student working at the intricacies of Greek grammar,
and reading it would give him a sense of accomplishment.
The last center fold of the grammar is occupied by another
suitable text, the *Laudatio in sanctissimam Dei Genetricem*,
again in both languages, evidence of Aldus' special devotion
to the Virgin, as a kind of final benediction.

Apparently Aldus' edition of Lascaris was well received,
for in another wholly new edition, printed in 1512, the same
general scheme is followed, including the interleaved Cebes
text. The last center fold contains *errata* discovered in the
Greek text. In a special note to the students he apologizes for
the mistakes and begs indulgence. He had hoped that in this
edition he could provide the reader with a vessel of gold or
silver, but unfortunately, because of the errors, it has proved
to be only earthenware.[18] His multiple activities have kept
him so busy night and day that he has not been able to
supervise the printing as he would have wished.[19] Yet, in
spite of this, so compelling was Aldus' enthusiasm for teaching that, after the regular grammar, he includes in this edition a new section of three and a half quires containing two
treatises, in Greek with his own translation, on the Greek
dialects.[20] This has in the center of the first text a small
treatise attributed to Plutarch on the dialects of Homer,
while *errata* fill the center fold of the other two quires. Then
he gives the order of the quires and directions to the binder.
The same appendix of Greek and the introduction to Hebrew
follow. At the end he bids farewell to the student and bids
him love him for his labors, as he believes he will.[21]

In another very ambitious work published by Aldus, the
*Poetae Christiani veteres*, one finds the same educational device of using the center pages of each quire, where the
Greek and Latin parallel texts are given, for an unrelated
text of moral or inspirational value.[22] Published in three
volumes in 1501, 1502, and 1504, this work is itself a labor
of love for the young students who will study it. Dedicating
it to his friend Daniele Clario of Parma who was teaching
at Ragusa, Aldus explains his purpose: "I have decided to

publish the Christian poets in the hope that the tender years of our children may be nurtured on them instead of the lying books of the heathen poets. Then, as young men, knowing how to distinguish the true from the false, they will be upright and truly Christian rather than wicked and faithless as many men are today."[23]

The first volume is divided into three parts which, apparently, might be printed separately. The greater part of the book is occupied with the Latin poetry of Prudentius. The following twenty-eight pages have the Latin epigrams of Prosper of Aquitaine. It is the third section containing the Greek hymns of Joannes Damascenus with a Latin translation where Aldus has used his unique device of intercalating an unrelated text in the center of the quire.[24] The hymns cover four quires and the center fold has the Greek and Latin text of the devotional work *In Annunciationem perquam sanctae Deiperae.* Volume Two is composed of the Latin poetry of Sedulius, Juvencus, and Arator, with the addition of the lives of St. Martin and St. Nicholas. The last five quires have the Greek text with the Latin translation of the *Homerocentra,* a cento of verses from Homer arranged to form a Christian epic. Here another text in honor of the Virgin, the *Ad Annunciationem purissimae Dei Genetricis,* is placed in the center fold. The third volume contains the Greek poems of Gregorius Nazianzenus with the Latin translation. The center pages are occupied with the Gospel according to St. John. This last text goes only to VI. 35. There follow fifty-one folios of the Greek text alone of Nonnus Panoplita's epic poem, a paraphrase of the Gospel of St. John. Aldus explains this unusual circumstance in his preface to the reader where he says that he had intended to make a Latin translation of the three thousand forty-seven verses of Nonnus, but the many demands upon his time prevented him from doing more than printing the Greek text.

A third work that Aldus arranged in such a way that either the Greek text or the Latin text might be printed sep-

arately or with parallel texts was his edition of the
Fables of Aesop, printed in 1505. Here again he took the
opportunity to print a different work in the facing center
folds of each quire. This time, however, since the various
treatises on mythology and fable that constitute the volume would indicate that it was directed to mature scholars,
the intercalated texts are not moralizing or devotional, but
rather supplementary material relevant to the main texts. So,
in the first center fold he printed *Ex Hermogenis exercitamen-
tis Prisciano interprete* and *Apologia Aesopi Phrygis memo-
ratu non inutilis.* The centers of the next three quires contain
the Greek and Latin of the Fables of the second-century writer
whom he calls Gabrias, now known as Babrius. With his
Greek text Aldus has difficulty as he explains in his preface.
He says that he had a very faulty model so there are many errors. When he found a corrected text, he thought it best to
print that immediately following the first so the reader could
correct it from the second. This text appears only in Greek
and it is consecutive. The rest of the volume is filled with
various treatises relating to mythology and the fable, and
all are printed in the conventional way.[25]

It is not solely in these volumes which Aldus so arranged
that the Greek text could be interleaved with the Latin
translation for the benefit of inexperienced students and
in so doing created an opportunity to present additional
texts of inspirational or instructional nature that the editor
shows his firm purpose to use his knowledge to further
the cause of education. Even though the very act of providing texts of the ancient authors constitutes a proof of
his constant encouragement to learning, his prefaces speak
specifically to his intent. In the introduction to one of his
early books, to justify his printing of Christian poets, he
reminds the reader that as the jar will always retain the
flavor of the wine that was first stored in it (Horace *Ep.*I.
2.70), so the mind of the adult will always hold the impression of the books that he read as a child. In the preface
of one of the last books he was able to see through the
press alone, the poems of Pindar, printed in 1515, he says,

"It is my intention to print and place in the hands of scholars the best works of the Greek and Latin writers, as I have often promised." At the same time he makes a commitment to print commentaries on Pindar, Hesiod, Sophocles, Aeschylus, Euripides, Theocritus, and Oppian, as well as an index for all the important topics for these as for all his other works, if only, a new Sisyphus, he can succeed in rolling his great stone to the summit of the hill. Unfortunately he did not live long enough to fulfill his ambition. One of his last books, his own Greek grammar, was published posthumously (1515) by Marcus Musurus, who, in a dedication to the great bibliophile, Jean Grolier, says of Aldus, "The noble man placed public interest above private consideration. Sparing no expense, never refusing any task, he lavished his resources and his very life in the interests of scholars." In view of his unswerving purpose to serve the intellectual, moral, and spiritual needs of students and scholars, it would seem a fair judgment to consider Aldus Manutius first a teacher, secondly an editor, and last of all a printer.[26]

# NOTES

## A Manuscript Fragment from Bede's Monastery

1. Quoted by Bede, *Historia ecclesiastica* II.1.

2. See Bede's *Historia abbatum*.

3. The history of the manuscript is given briefly by E. A. Lowe, *English Uncials* (Oxford, 1969), pp. 7-13.

4. See J. W. Thompson, *The Medieval Library* (Chicago, 1939), p. 111.

5. See E. A. Lowe, "A Key to Bede's Scriptorium," *Scriptorium*, XII (1958), pp. 184-185.

6. I am indebted to Professor Bernhard Bischoff for this identification. See P. Lehmann, *Nordisk Tidskrift för Bok-och Biblioteksväsen*, XXII (1935), pp. 116-126.

7. A manuscript in Munich (6278) was written in the eighth century.

8. The Itala version reads *habeam*, while the Vulgate has *habuero*.

9. Cf. Epistolae, ed. P. Jaffé, *Bibliotheca Rerum Germanicarum*, III: *Monumenta Moguntiana*, p. 250.

## A Manuscript of Charlemagne's
### *Homiliarium*

1. The text is given in F. Wiegand, *Das Homiliarium Karls des Grossen* (Leipzig, 1897), pp. 15-16

2. See C. Cipolla, "Note bibliografiche . . . delle opere di Paolo Diacono," *Miscellanea di Storia Veneta*, VIII (1902), pp. 10-12.

3. No. 21 (xq.264.6.P.28h), De Ricci, *Census I*, 703. See W. A. Old-father and I. G. Lough, "The Urbana MS of the Homiliarium of Paulus Diaconus," *Speculum*, VI (1931), pp. 293-295.

4. See J. Leclercq, "Tables pour l'inventaire des Homiliaires manu-scrits," *Scriptorium*, II (1948), pp. 205-214.

# A Bifolium from a *Sacramentarium Gregorianum*

1. E. M. Thompson, *Introduction to Greek and Latin Palaeography* (Oxford, 1912) pp. 64-66, gives an impressive list of early works preserved in palimpsests.

2. These, of course, do not include the large manuscripts, often anti-phonaries, that were wantonly dismembered in the eighteenth and nine-teenth centuries to provide attractive covers for books.

3. They are rather casual notes that seem to add nothing to the under-standing of the text; neither do they provide a clue as to the provenance of the manuscript.

4. Edited by C. L. Feltoe, Cambridge, 1896.

5. Edited by H. A. Wilson, Oxford, 1894.

6. See H. A. Wilson, *The Gregorian Sacramentary* (London, 1915).

7. Ibid., 223.

8. Ibid., 221.

9. Ibid., 222.

10. Ibid., 229-230.

11. Ibid., 229.

12. See H. A. Wilson, *The Gelasian Sacramentary*, pp. 111-112.

13. H. A. Wilson, *The Gregorian Sacramentary*, p. 229.

14. Ibid., 230.

15. *The Roman Ritual*, edited and translated by P. T. Weller (Mil-waukee, 1952), II, pp. 186-187.

## A Medieval Textbook

1. Edited by Edmond Faral, *Les arts poétiques du XII$^e$ et du XIII$^e$ siècle* (Paris, 1962), pp. 336-377.

2. For a discussion of the "curriculum authors," see E.R. Curtius, *European Literature and the Latin Middle Ages* (New York, 1953), pp. 48-54.

3. The only modern text of Theodulus is that edited by J. Osternacher (Urfahr, 1902).

4. See R.B.C. Huygens, *Accessus ad Auctores, Bernard d'Utrecht, Conrad d'Hirsau, Dialogus super auctores* (Leyden, 1970), pp. 55-69.

5. Yale has two incunable editions of Theodulus with commentaries. The first, published in 1487 at Lyons, has a commentary by Odo Picardus. The second, *Ecloga cum commentario*, was published in Cologne by Henricus Quentell in 1495.

6. See Avianus, *Oeuvres*, edited by L. Herrmann (Brussels, 1968), pp. 27-28.

7. Edited by R. Webster (New York, 1900) and recently by T. Agozzino (Bologna, 1970).

8. *Registrum multorum auctorum*, edited by K. Langosch (Darmstadt, 1942) 1.612.

9. See R.B.C. Huygens, *Accessus ad Auctores*, p. 25.

10. *Doctrinale*, lines 3-4 (Marston MS 64).

11. Edited by E. Voigt (Halle, 1889).

## Johannes Climacus' *Ladder* of *Divine Ascent*

1. *St. John Climacus, the Ladder of Divine Ascent*, translated by Archimandrite Lazarus Moore (London, 1959), Step. 15.89.

2. The Greek text is published in Migne, *P. G.* LXXXVIII. 632-1164. 632-1164.

3. See John R. Martin, *The Illustration of the Heavenly Ladder of John Climacus* (Princeton, 1954).

4. See "The Ziskind Collection of Greek Manuscripts" in the Yale University Library *Gazette* XXXII (1958), pp. 38-56.

5. See H.R. Wagner, *Nueva bibliografia mexicana del siglo XVI* (Mexico, 1940), 5-8, 508.

## Walter Burley's
### De Vita et Moribus Philosophorum

1. See P. Labbé, *Biblioteca Bibliotecarum* (Rouen, 1678), p. 17.

2. C.F. Bühler has discussed the influence of Burley's book in his *Early Books and Manuscripts* (New York, 1973), pp. 341-352.

3. For details of Burley's life, see T.A. Archer's article in *DNB*, VII (1886) pp. 374-376, and R. Wedler "Walter Burley's *Liber de vita et moribus philosophorum poetarumque veterum*" in *Zwei deutschen Bearbeitungen des Spätmittelalters* (Karlsruhe, 1969) pp. 2-12.

4. G. Sarton, *Introduction to the History of Science* (Baltimore, 1947), III, 564.

5. I wish to thank Barbara Shailor for her help in detecting these books.

6. See H. Knust, *Gualteri Burlaei Liber de Vita et Moribus Philosophorum* (Tubingen, 1886), p. 144.

## The Apocryphal Abgarus-Jesus Epistles
## in England in the Middle Ages

1. Abgarus V who reigned from A.D. 13 to A.D. 50.

2. The most complete treatment of the letters is found in E. von Dobschütz, "Der Briefwechsel zwischen Abgar und Jesus," *Zeitschrift für wissenschaftliche Theologie*, XLIII (1900), pp. 422-486.

3. These additions are discussed by L.J. Tixeront, *Les Origines de l'Eglise d'Edesse et la Légende d'Abgar* (Paris, 1888). The Greek text of the *Acta Thaddaei* is given by M. Bonnet and R. A. Lipsius, *Acta Apostolorum Apocrypha* (Leipzig, 1891), pp. 273-278.

4. This occurs in the sixth-century *Passio Thomae*. The text is given in E. von Dobschütz, *Christusbilder* (Leipzig, 1899), p. *181.

5. See the edition of H. Pétré (Paris, 1948), pp. 163-171.

6. Aetheria gives as an illustration of the power of the letters the fact that once a Persian army, ready to attack, was turned away from the gates of Edessa when the letters were exposed. See Pétré, *op. cit.*, pp. 167-169.

7. The manuscript was discovered in a convent at Arezzo in 1884 by J.F. Gamurrini, who published it in 1887.

8. Apart from Aetheria's account, in early Latin literature of the Middle Ages there is only a slight reference to the letter of Abgarus to Jesus in a letter written by Comes Darius to St. Augustine about 429. See Augustinus, *Ep.* 230 (*P.L.*XXXIII, 1022).

9. See Eusebius Caesariensis *Historia ecclesiastica* latine Rufino Aquileiensi interprete (Utrecht, 1474), I. capita XVI-SVIII.

10. The existence of the letters in Edessa is corroborated by an Eastern source, the *History of Armenia* written by Moses of Chorene in the fifth century. See the edition and French translation of P.E. Le Vaillant (Paris, 184?) I. Book II, pp. 217-223.

11. A modern translation of Eusebius is that of R.J. Deferrari (N.Y., 1953). The Abgarus legend occurs on pp. 76-82.

12. See *Oxford Dictionary of the Christian Church* (London, 1963) p.5. For a discussion of the attacks on the authenticity of the letters as well as for their supporters, see Dobschütz, *Der Briefwechsel* pp. 485-487.

13. The text of the *Decretum* is given in E. von Dobschütz, "Das Decretum Gelasianum de libris recipiendis et non recipiendis," in A. Harnack and C. Schmidt, *Texte und Untersuchungen zur altchristlichen Literatur*, XXXVIII (1912), pp. 13, 319.

14. See M.R. James, *The Apocryphal New Testament* (Oxford, 1926), pp. 476-477.

15. See the edition of Hagenau, Joannes Secerius (1531) Book II, cap. III.

16. British Museum, Cottonian Library, Julius E VII, f. 136.

17. British Musuem, Royal MS 2Axx, f. 12a.

18. See W.B. Skeat, *Aelfric's Lives of the Saints* (London, 1900), II, pp. 59-66.

19. See Ordericus Vitalis, *Ecclesiasticae Historiae Libri XIII*, ed. A. LeProvost (Paris, 1838), I, Book II, p. 319; III, Book IX, pp. 564-565.

20. Gervasius of Tilbury, *Otia imperialia*, Dec. III, 23 in G.W. Leibnitz, *Scriptores rerum Brunsvicensium* (Hanover, 1707), I, pp. 966-967.

21. Vincentius Bellovacensis, *Speculum historiale* (Venice, 1494), VII, 29-30.

22. See *P.L.* XCVIII, 1256.

23. See *Legenda aurea* (Strassburg, 1481), CLII De Symone et Iuda Apostolis.

24. See William Caxton, *The Golden Legend*, reprinted by the Kelmscott Press, 1892, ed. F.S. Ellis, III, pp. 965-967.

25. It is unusual to find the first letter without the second, for, of course, it is the reply of Jesus that Christians valued.

26. How widely these letters were distributed in England is suggested by a curious note on the use of the second letter as a kind of phylactery. Writing in 1798, Jeremiah Jones says, "The common people of England have it in their houses, in many places, fixed in a frame with our Saviour's picture before it; and they generally with much honesty and devotion regard it as the word of God, and the genuine Epistle of Christ." (*New and Full Method of settling the Canonical Authority of the New Testament*, p.2). In his *Ancient Syriac Documents* (p. 155), W. Cureton remarks, "I have a recollection of having seen the same thing in cottages in Shropshire." Neil Ker tells me that he has recently seen a thirteenth-century copy of the Jesus letter on a single sheet of magic and charms now in Canterbury Cathedral, MS Add. 23.

# A Fourteenth-Century Argument for an
# International Date Line

1. Antonio Pigafetta, *Magellan's Voyage: A Narrative Account of the First Circumnavigation.* . . . Translated and edited by R. A. Skelton (New Haven and London, 1969) I, 147-148. (The reverse of Pigafetta's experience is familiar to all from Jules Verne's tale of an adventurous trip eastward around the world in 80 days. When the punctual Phileas Fogg, owner of numerous complex chronometers, returned to London on what he believed was Saturday, 21 December, he found to his surprise that it was actually Friday the twentieth and that he had won the famous wager at the Reform Club.)

2. I have found no other copy of this Latin treatise.

3. Pierre d'Ailly, *Ymago mundi*, ed. Edmond Buron (Paris, 1930), see especially vol. I.

4. V.P. Zoubov, "Un voyage imaginaire autour du monde au XIV$^e$ siècle," *Congresso International de Historia des Descobrimentos, Actas* II (1961), pp. 563-573.

5. This has been edited with a translation by A.D. Menut and A.J. Denomy as *Nicole Oresme. Le livre du ciel et du monde* (Madison, 1968).

6. *Ibid.*, p. 579.

7. *Commentary on the Dream of Scipio*, Chapter X, section 20.

8. The most recent treatment of the life of Oresme is that by R. Mathieu in *Dictionnaire des lettres françaises, IV: Le Moyen Age* (Paris, 1964), pp. 549-552.

9. G. Sarton *(Introduction to the History of Science,* III 2, 1495) would qualify the earlier claims that Oresme actually formulated the famous law.

10. Cf. Pierre Duhem, "Un précurseur français de Copernic, Nicole Oresme," *Revue générale des sciences pures et appliquées,* XX (1909), pp. 866-873. Sarton *(History of Science,* III 2, p. 1490) says, "It is not quite correct to call him a forerunner of Copernicus, but he prepared the way for the Copernican revolution."

11. For a modern estimate of this claim, see D.B. Durand, "Nicole Oresme and the Mediaeval Origins of Modern Science," *Speculum,* XVI (1941), pp. 170-175.

12. Zoubov, "*Un voyage imaginaire,*", p. 568.

## Note on St. Basil's
### Address on Reading Greek Literature

1. *St. Odo of Cluny* translated and edited by Dom Gerard Sitwell (New York, 1958), p. 14.

2. *Epistola* XXII. 30.

3. *De Doctrina Christiana* II. 40.

4. *Confessiones* III. 4.

5. Evidence contradictory to this generalization is given by Dom Jean Leclerq in *The Love of Learning and the Desire for God*, translated by C. Mistahi (New York, 1961), pp. 116-151.

6. The best modern edition is that of R.J. Deferrari and M.R.P. McGuire (Cambridge, 1934). See Vol. IV, pp. 365-435.

7. L. Schucan in *Das Nachleben von Basilius Magnus "ad adolescentes"* (Geneva, 1973), p. 43; on pp. 233-235 he lists 22 manuscripts, apart from those that contain all the *Homiliae*, that were written in the East.

8. Bruni would appear to be protesting against such scholars as Giuliano Zonarini, chancellor of Bologna, and Giovanni Dominici, vicar general of the Dominican Order, who expressed his views in *Lucula Noctis*. (ed. E. Hunt, Notre Dame, 1940, especially pp. 147-432). B.L. Ullman (*The Humanism of Coluccio Salutati*, Padua, 1963, pp. 39-49) gives an account of Coluccio's controversy with these men.

9. See Schucan, *Das Nachleben*, pp. 235-242.

10. See *loc. cit.*, pp. 244-245.

11. Translated and edited by W.H. Woodward, *Vittorino da Feltre and other Humanist Educators* (Cambridge, 1897), p. 133.

12. Ibid., p. 150.

13. In this volume the *Address* is printed with the *Homiliae*, pp. 403-413.

14. See L.K. Born, *The Education of a Christian Prince by Desiderius Erasmus* (New York, 1936), p. 150.

15. It is known that in 1638 Milton was introduced to Grotius. One finds an echo of the *Address* in Milton's account of Satan's temptation of Christ (*Paradise Regained* IV. 225-229):

> All knowledge is not couched in Moses' law,
> The Pentateuch or what the Prophets wrote;
> The Gentiles also know and write, and teach
> To admiration, led by Nature's light;
> With the Gentiles much must thou converse.

16. Schucan, *Das Nachleben*, pp. 244-247, lists 117 editions in Greek or Latin to the year 1625.

## Aesticampianus' Edition of the *Tabula*
## Attributed to Cebes

1. *Cf.* H. Grimm, *Neue Deutsche Biographie* (Berlin, 1953) I, 92-93.

2. Aesticampianus mentions this in an introductory letter to his text.

3. *Cf.* Aulus Gellius, *Noctes Atticae*, II, 18.

4. It is first mentioned by Lucian in the second century (*cf. De mercede conductis*, 42, and *Rhetorum praeceptor*, 6). Tertullian also mentions the dialogue, which he says a relative of his had paraphrased in Latin verse (*cf. De praescriptione haereticorum*, Ch. xxxix).

5. *Cf. Memorabilia*, II,I,21-34. It is retold by Cicero, *De officiis*, I,32. S.C. Chew, in his *The Pilgrimage of Life* (New Haven, 1962), 174-181, considers the representations of this tale.

6. There were subsequent printings in 1500 and 1503.

7. The Beinecke Library has copies of these two editions as well as the 1557 edition printed by Aldus' son Paulus.

8. The boast that Aesticampianus was the first to introduce the *Tabula* to the lands north of the Alps is true only in the very strictest sense, for Odaxius' Latin translation was printed in Paris by Guy Marchant in 1498. There is a copy of this in the Beinecke Library.

9. This information is supplied by J.A. Fabricius in his *Biblioteca Latina Mediae et Infimae Aetatis* (Hamburg, 1736), V/VI, 198-202.

10. Letter I, 17 relates the story of Aesticampianus' difficulties and his eventual expulsion (*Cf. Epistolae obscurorum virorum*, ed. F. G. Stokes (London, 1925), pp. 47-51).

11. For the most nearly complete listing of the editions see S.F.W. Hoffmann, *Bibliographisches Lexicon der Griechen* (Amsterdam, 1961)— a reprint of the Leipzig 1838-45 edition—I, 438-48. Among these, the first critical edition by H. Wolf, printed in Basel in 1560 and reprinted many times, is one of the most noteworthy, and the first to raise the question of the authorship of the dialogue.

12. This is reproduced as fig. 50, p. 50, in H. Knackfuss, *Holbein*, tr. by C. Dodgson (Bielefeld and Leipzig, 1899).

13. This is not the Odaxius translation and there is no indication of the translator. Aldus used this translation in his edition of Cebes printed in the Lascaris *Erotemata* in the editions of 1494-95, 1501-2, and 1557. It was also used in an edition published in Antwerp in 1547.

14. The text attracted some of the greatest philologists, *e.g.* Gronovius, who published an edition in 1689 in Amsterdam.

15. Yale has a copy of this unusual text. Since the Greek text is incomplete, many of the Latin translators used the Arabic to supply the ending.

16. See "Letter to Master Samuel Hartlib on Education" in *The Works of John Milton*, Columbia edition (New York, 1931), IV.281.

17. See Fabricius, *Bibliotheca*, p. 198.

## Aesticampianus' Commentary on the
### *De Grammatica* of Martianus Capella

1. *An English Miscellany,* Presented to Dr. Furnivall in Honour of his Seventy-fifth Birthday (Oxford, 1901), p. 1.

2. Book III, p. 231 (p. 86, 11. 5-6 in the edition of A. Dick [Leipzig, 1925]). All references will be to Dick's edition.

3. This occurs at the end of Book IX. Among the manuscripts that preserve this addition, I note Cambridge, Corpus Christi College 153, fol. 67$^v$, a manuscript of the ninth century, and Oxford, Merton College 291, fol. 94$^v$, a manuscript of the twelfth century.

4. Cf. C.E. Lutz, "Remigius' ideas on the classification of the seven liberal arts," *Traditio* XII (1956), 78-84.

5. Cf. C.E. Lutz, *Remigii Autissiodorensis Commentum in Martianum Capellam Libri I-II* (Leyden, 1962), pp. 23-24.

6. *Martiani Minei Felicis Capellae Carthaginiensis Satyricon* (Leyden, 1599). He calls his exegesis *Februa in Satyricon Martiani Capellae.*

7. *Grammatica Martiani Foelicis Capellae cum Iohannis Rhagii Aesticampiani Rhetoris et poete prefatione.* Impressa Frankophordio per honestos viros Nicolaum Lamperter et Balthasar Murrer. Anno Domini MDVII. I am using a microfilm copy of the book which is now in the Universitätsbibliothek in Munich. It bears the shelfmark 4° A. lat. 46. It has sixty-one pages.

8. Martianus' representations of the arts determined their iconography throughout the Middle Ages and the Renaissance. Cf. R. van Marle, *Iconographie de l'art profane au Moyen-Age et à la Renaissance* (La Haye, 1932) II, pp. 203-279.

9. Ulrici Hutteni ad studiosos adulescentes de liberalibus studiis Elegiaca exhortatio.

10. *Commentarii Iohannis Rhagii Aesticampiani Rhetoris et poetae laureati in Grammaticam Martiani Capellae et Donati figuras.* Impressa Frankophordio per honestos viros Nicolaum Lamperter et Balthasar Murrer. Anno Domini MDVIII. It is eighty-six pages long. This text was listed under its full title in J.A. Fabricius, *Bibliotheca Latina Mediae et Infimae Aetatis,* VI (Hamburg, 1736), 201, but it has long been thought a mere ghost. Happily, two copies were tracked down by Dr. Emilie Boer of the Deutsche Akademie der Wissenschaften zu Berlin. One is in Munich in the Bayerische Staatsbibliothek with the shelfmark 4° L. lat. 426; the other is in the Sächsische Landesbibliothek at Dresden with the shelfmark Lit. 6. rom. B. 1806. I am using a microfilm of the latter. I wish to express my thanks to Dr. Boer for her very generous help in locating the books, and to the Sächsische Landesbibliothek for permitting me to study and to quote from the book.

For the commentaries on Martianus Capella, see my article in *Catalogus Translationum et Commentariorum,* vol. II, ed. P.O. Kristeller and F.E.

Cranz (Washington, 1971) 367-381. I discovered the Aesticampianus commentary while I was preparing this article, although too late for inclusion.

11. P. 2: "Facturum me, Nepotes dulcissimi, rem et vobis iucundam et ceteris quoque iuvenibus pergratam arbitror, si et obscuritatem et ieiunitatem Capellae nostri quibusdam in locis quam brevissimis tum graecorum tum latinorum vocabulorum annotamentis, ita ut quaeque mihi notatu digna occurrent, obiter illustrem et paululum exatiem."

12. P. 3: "Ut rudibus pueris monstratur littera primum
Per faciem nomenque suum componitur usus;
Tunc coniuncta suis formatur syllaba nodis;
Hinc verbis structura venit per verba ligandi,
Tunc rerum vires atque artis traditur usus,
Inque pedes proprios nascentia carmina surgunt;
Singulaque in summa prodest didicisse priora."

*Astr.* II. 755-761

13. P. 3. This material is taken largely from Herodotus, *Hist.* V. 58, Pliny, *H.N.* VII. 56, Tacitus, *Ann.* XI. 14, and Lucan, *Bellum Civile* III. 220.

14. I have not located the source of these verses. Cornelius Agrippa von Nettesheim (1486-1535) in his *De incertitudine et vanitate scientiarum declamatio*, in ch. 2, says that he found the verses in "pervetusto codice," and he quotes them. Joannes Brassicanus of Tübingen (fl. 1508), in his *Institutiones grammaticae*, quotes the lines without naming his source. Petrus Crinitus (1465-1504), in his *De honesta disciplina* (Basel, 1536), Lib. XVII, pp. 250-251, does indeed mention finding the verses "in pervetusto codice ex biblioteca septimana" and repeats them.

15. P. 9. Commenting upon Martianus 87. 4 *Y velut Greca reiecta*, he gives as his source the *Littera Pythagorae* which the Middle Ages attributed to Virgil.

16. 16. P. 10: "Inventa autem est y a Palamede cum grues
videret volare. Mar.
'Turbabis versus nec littera tota volabit
Unam perdideris si Palamedis avem.'"

Martial XIII. 75-76

17. P. 14.
18. P. 15.
19. P. 7.
20. P. 7.
21. P. 7. He quotes the *De Oratore* I, 42, 187: "In grammaticis poetarum pertractatio, historiarum cognitio, verborum interpretatio, pronuntiandi quidam sonus requiritur."
22. P. 8. Cf. G. Funaioli, *Grammaticae Romanae Fragmenta* (Stuttgart, 1969), p. 266 (no. 236).
23. P. 8. One has the impression that Aesticampianus was commenting upon Martianus with one eye upon Donatus. For example, on p. 37 he

says, "Declinationes eorundem et hic Martianus insinuat et Donatus aperte explicat."

24. This is, of course, the traditional division.

25. P. 60: "De supino vel participiali in um Martianus noster tacet."

26. P. 71.

27. P. 66: "De constructione pluribus agam, Nepotes studiosissimi, ne fúndamentis grammatice que sunt in litteris, syllabis, dictionibusque artificiose positis ipsa oratio quasi aedificium quoddam structure totius magnificum deesse videatur."

28. E.g., p. 66: "Vocalis vel substantialis ut sum vel vocor Joannes. . . . ut doceo grammaticam. . . . Posco te librum meum. Doceo te litteras; tu doceris a me litteras."

29. 86. 7.

30. P. 5. Cf. *De Grammaticis* 4.

31. P. 84. Cf. Terence, *Andria* I, 2, 23.

32. P. 21. Cf. Suetonius, *Deperditorum librorum reliquiae*, ed. C.L. Roth, p. 296.

33. P. 26: "Ut Serenus parva sabucus item hircino condita sevo"; cf. Quinti Sereni *Liber Medicinalis*, ed. F. Vollmer (Corpus Medicorum Latinorum, vol. II, fasc. 3), Leipzig, 1916, ch. XLI, 1. 780.

34. P. 4: "At divus martyr Cyprianus Saturnum in latium eas primum tulisse ac imprimere docuisse." Cf. Cyprianus, *Quod idola dii non sint*, 2 in his *Opera*, ed. G. Hartel (Corpus Scriptorum Ecclesiasticorum Latinorum, vol. 3, pt. 1) Vienna, 1868, p. 20.

35. P. 9: "Papyrianus refert harmoniam litterariam esse vim litterarum que auribus inspiretur." I have not located this reference.

36. P. 60: "unde fatisco que Valla meditativa seu exercitativa appellat." Cf. Lorenzo Valla, *Elegantiarum Libri VI* (Venice, 1536), pp. 24$^b$ and 25$^a$.

37. P. 6. He begins with a distich parodying the end of 49:

> "Tantum parva suo debet Verona Catullo
> Quantum magna suo Mantua Virgilio."

He then quotes all of 49 and 6 lines of 14.

38. P. 20. He cites Statius and Eusebius as his sources.

39. P. 22.

40. P. 20.

41. P. 23.

42. P. 20.

43. P. 20.

44. P. 4. Cf. Augustinus, *De doctrina Christiana* II. 11.

45. 149, 18 to 150, 13.

46. P. 77: "Et ego quoque eandem commentariolis meis tanquam pedissequis quibusdam, si deus voluerit, comitabor quos et vobis, Nepotes optimi, legendos esse censeo." In 1509 Aesticampianus published Martianus' *De Rhetorica*, and at the end of his text he added: "Commentarios

Aesticampiani tui diligens lector expecta." So far as I know, he never fulfilled this promise.

47. Pp. 77-84, Cf. Donatus, *Ars grammatica* (Keil, *Grammatici Latini* IV. 392-394).

48. P. 84: "Ita perspicue et breviter Donatus noster loquitur ut vix aliquid quo minus vel obscurior vel prolixior reddatur adduci potest."

49. P. 84.

50. P. 85.

51. P. 86, where he is paraphrasing Horace, *C.* I. 7. 25-26.

52. P. 86: "Ergo brevi vades, ne te via longa moretur,
          Calle; per hunc petulans ire Capella solet,
     Cuius hic interpres vepreta recondita purgat;
          Falce nova tritam te iubet ire viam."

53. Christopher Manlius, *Lusatiae Liber VII De viris illustribus,* in C. G. Hoffman, *Scriptores rerum Lusaticarum,* I (Leipzig, 1719), 435.

54. *Ibid.*, 434-436.

55. J.A. Fabricius, *Bibliotheca Latina Mediae et Infimae Aetatis,* VI (Hamburg, 1736), 198-202; *Neue Deutsche Biographie,* I (1953), 92-93 (by H. Grimm); K. Schottenloher, *Bibliographie zur deutschen Geschichte im Zeitalter der Glaubensspaltung,* I (1933), nos. 96-103; G. Bauch, "Johannes Rhagius Aesticampianus," *Archiv fuer Litteraturgeschichte,* 12 (1884), 321-370.

56. This is given in full by Manlius and in an abbreviated version in Fabricius.

## Bishop Dubravius on Fishponds

1. There is a copy of this book in the Beinecke Rare Book and Manuscript Library of Yale University.

2. See his "Epilogue," leaf 37 verso.

3. See P. Lehmann, *Eine Geschichte der alten Fuggerbibliotheken* (Tübingen, 1960) II, pp. 15-16.

4. The Beinecke Library has a fifteenth-century manuscript (MS 233) of this work, the gift of Mrs. David Wagstaff in 1952.

5. See leaves 35 verso and 36 recto.

6. The Beinecke Library has a fifteenth-century manuscript of this work (MS. 171), given by Mrs. David Wagstaff in 1947.

7. See *The Anatomy of Melancholy,* ed. H. Jackson (New York, 1932), II, 73.

8. See *The Complete Angler,* ed. John Major (New York, 1925), pp. 182-183.

## A Diamond and a Dürer in Dubravius'
## Commentary on Martianus Capella

1. *Martianus Foelix Capella de Nuptiis Mercurii et Philologiae, cum Adnotationibus Ioannis Dubravii.* One of the few copies of this book still extant is in the Beinecke Library.

2. I am most grateful to Margaret Eschler for her help in tracing the diamond.

3. See Götz Freiherr von Pölnitz, *Jakob Fugger* (Tübingen, 1949) I, 51-59.

4. *Ibid.*, II.23.

5. Paul Lehmann in *Eine Geschichte der alten Fuggerbibliotheken* (Tübingen, 1960) p. 14, quotes a long preface in which Dubravius speaks of being invited to Pannonia to the country estate of Anton Fugger, a great house that once belonged to Constantia, wife of King Ottokar of Bohemia.

6. See *Jacob Fugger the Rich* by Jacob Strieder, translated by M.L. Hartsough (New York, 1966), p. 103.

7. See N. Lieb, *Die Fugger und die Kunst* (Munich, 1952), p. 82.

8. *Ibid.*, p. 82.

9. See A. Weitnauer, *Venezianischer Handel der Fugger* (Munich and Leipzig, 1931), p. 103.

10. *Diarii di Marino Sanuto*, ed. N. Barozzi (Venice, 1882), VIII, 87-88.

11. See G. von Pölnitz, *Jakob Fugger*, II, 211.

12. There may, of course, be a simple prosaic explanation. It is known that Cardinal Melchior de Cupis, Bishop of Brixen, had 300,000 florins invested with the Fuggers. Upon his death on 27 March 1509, Julius II may have taken the diamond as part payment in the settlement of the estate. Commenting on the wealth of the Cardinal, Martin Luther in his *Tischreden* (Cap. 4.88, ed. J.G. Walch, St. Louis, 1877, XXII, p. 217) makes some provocative remarks on the sudden death of Melchior, the unusual circumstances of the discovery of a letter of credit on the Fuggers sewn into his sleeve, and the fact that his will was contested.

13. Parides De Grassis, the master of ceremonies under Julius II and Leo X, records in his manuscript Journal for 4 February 1513 (quoted by J. Klaczko, *Rome and the Renaissance* (New York, 1903), p. 362) that the Pope, during his last illness, called him to his bedroom and asked him to take care of his funeral and to put on his hand two of his most precious rings. In view of this request, it would not be surprising if the valuable cope also was buried with him. If this was the case, it must have been lost when, in 1527, during the sack of Rome, the coffin of Julius was robbed.

14. E. Panofsky, *Albrecht Dürer* (Princeton, 1943), I, 119. Most of these studies are reproduced in Volume II.

15. Panofsky, *Dürer*, II, no. 117.

16. Panofsky, *Dürer*, II, nos. 164 & 165.

17. The Latin original is quoted in H. Rupprich, *Dürer Schriftlicher Nachlass* (Berlin, 1956), I, 296.

18. H. Rupprich, *Dürer*, I, 67-68.

19. Joachim von Sandrarts *Academie der Bau- Bilder- und Mahlerey-Kunste von 1675*, edited by A.R. Peltzer (Munich, 1925), chap. 3, p. 66.

20. H. Tietze and E. Tietze-Conrat, *Kritisches Verzeichnis der Werke Albrecht Dürers* (Basel & Leipzig, 1937), II:1.38.

# The *Theriobulia* of Jan Dubravius

1. *Oesterreichisches Archiv für Geschichte, Erdbeschreibung, Staatenkunde, Kunst und Literatur*, I (1831), 294-296, 302-304, 316.

2. Vol. IX, p. 547. no. 155b.

3. Typ 520.20.340.

4. See "Life and Writings of Dubravius, Bishop of Olmütz (1542-1553)," by Albert H. Wratislaw, in *Transactions of the Royal Historical Society*, IX, series I (1881), 148.

5. Louis (1506-1526) had already been crowned King of Hungary in 1508 and of Bohemia in 1509.

6. The cousin furnishes this information in the dedicatory epistle.

7. The word appears to have been coined by Dubravius from Θηρίον and βουλή.

8. For a discussion of this work, see Albert H. Wratislaw, *The Native Literature of Bohemia in the Fourteenth Century* (Four Lectures Delivered before the University of Oxford on the Ilchester Foundation) London, 1878, pp. 60-65; J. Feifalik, "Studien zur Geschichte der altböhmischen Literatur," *Oesterreichische Akademie der Wissenschaften, Sitzungsberichte, Philosophisch-historische Classe* (Prague, 1937), pp. 1-53. I am greatly indebted to Halyna Lobay for translating this last work.

9. Feifalik (*Studien*, pp. 694-696) argues for an earlier date, namely 1378 or 1379, when Wenceslaus was seventeen years old.

10. Feifalik (*Studien*, pp. 696-700) treats this work.

11. On the other hand, the phoenix speaks in Dubravius' poem.

12. For an account of his writings, see A. Truhlář and C. Hradina, *Enchiridion renatae poesis Latinae in Bohemia et Moravia cultae* (Prague, 1966) II, 74-84.

13. I shall cite only a few from the dozens of instances of the use of classical echoes:

    (1) Dove—Non si mihi linguae centum sint, oraque/ Centum, nec ipsa vox adesset ferrea (cf. Virgil, *Georgics* II.43.)

    (2) Goose—Gortynia spicula (cf. Virgil, *Aeneid* XI.773).

    (3) Crow—Moeror quasi ipso Calvitio queat/ Levarier (cf. Cicero, *Tusc. Disp.* III.26.62).

    (4) Fox—regiae Gazae (cf. Cicero, *De Imp. Pomp.* 23.66)

    (5) Fox—Novi ego eos Polypos, qui ubi quid/ Tangunt, tenere id perpetuo sciunt (cf. Plautus, *Aulularia* II.2.21).

    (6) Lark—quae si memorem ego. . . . diem/ Nox adimat (cf. Plautus, *Captivi* II.3.56).

    (7) Flamingo—Invita ut facias nihil/ Ac pugnante Minerva (cf. Horace, *Ars Poetica* 385).

    (8) Elephant—alma faustitas (cf. Horace, *Odes* IV.5.18).

    (9) Prologue to Book II—prono tonderent gramina morsu/ Gramina gemmatis passim rorantia guttis (cf. Lucretius, *De rerum natura* II.319).

  (10) Deer—montivagae . . . Dammulae (cf. Lucretius, *De rerum natura* I.404).

  (11) Phoenix—Hinc nata ad auroram, Nabathaeaque / Ad regna Phoenix (cf. Ovid, *Met.* I.61).

  14. Book XII, Epistle II.

## Manuscripts Copied from Printed Books

1. C.F. Bühler, *The Fifteenth-Century Book* (Philadelphia, 1960), p. 41.

2. Tam longum tandem finisti penna laborem.

3. *Epistolae familares* XVIII.12. See also his *De librorum copia*, p. 35, ed. C. H. Rawski (Cleveland, 1967).

4. *The Works of Geoffrey Chaucer*, ed. F. N. Robinson (Boston, 1957), p. 534.

5. See J. Destrez, *La Pecia dans les manuscrits universitaires* (Paris, 1935).

6. Besides the usual marks in the margins to indicate where quires of the original ended, at the foot of f. 110$^r$, a note partly cut off reads: Incipit in xli pecia . . . .

7. Nota: confundatur stationarius qui me fecit deturpari librum alicuius probi viri. See E. T. Silk, "The Fletcher Manuscript of St. Thomas on the 'Sentences' of Peter Lombard," Yale University Library *Gazette*, XXV (1951), pp. 60-62

8. Very noteworthy is the stand taken by Johannes Trithemius, abbot of Sponheim, who, in 1492, wrote a treatise *De laude scriptorum*. In it he urges all monks to continue copying important works, both those in manuscripts and those already printed, for, he argues, vellum will last a thousand years, but paper may not last more than two hundred. Cf. edition of R. Behrendt(Lawrence, Kansas, 1974), pp. 62-65.

9. T. E. Marston has called attention to this in his article, "A Note on the Printing of Incunabula," Yale University Library *Gazette*, XXXIX (1964), p. 83.

10. C. F. Bühler, *The Fifteenth Century Book*, pp. 34-39, has discussed this question and given many examples of it.

11. *Gesamtkatalog der Wiegendrucke* 6790.

12. The manuscript copy follows the four printed texts. After it eight more folios contain two short treatises in manuscript: Joannes Andreae, *Super arboribus consanguinitatis, affinitatis, et cognationis* and *Summa de sponsalibus et matrimoniis*.

13. In this volume the manuscript occurs between the fourth and fifth printed treatises, not one of which was printed in Augsburg.

14. The first treatise is complete on ff. $52^r$ to $56^r$ in Lambarde. The second begins on f. $134^r$ and continues to $139^v$, then goes back to $128^v$ and ends at $130^v$. The beginning is lacking.

15. *A Catalogue of an extensive and extraordinary Assemblage of the Productions of the Aldine Press,* published by James Toovey in London in 1880, lists Renouard's own copy of the *editio princeps* of the Musaeus in Greek and Latin as one bound in blue morocco by Bozérian.

16. See S. De Ricci, *English Collectors of Books and Manuscripts (New* York, 1930), p. 159.

17. C. F. Bühler has discussed the Aldine edition of this text in an article, "Aldus Manutius and his First Edition of the Greek Musaeus," *Early Books and Manuscripts* (New York, 1973), pp. 162-169.

18. Julius Caesar Scaliger, *Poetices libri septem* (Geneva, 1561), p. 5.

19. He says, "It is my wish that the oldest poet, Musaeus, take precedence over Aristotle and the other philosophers whom I intend to print soon, and that because the little poem is at the same time the most charming and the most eloquent."

20. Although Leander's body is lying on the shore, there is also the figure of a man swimming, much like that in the first woodcut. It is interesting to note that in the 1517 edition the swimming man does not appear and the sea is represented as very rough.

21. Suidas, *Lexicon* 1294-1297, ed. A. Adler (Leipzig, 1926), III, pp. 415-416.

22. See Bühler, *The Fifteenth-Century Book*, pp. 165-167.

23. The British Museum copy (1A 24387) which has only the Greek text does not have the title page, but Bühler reports that one of the Vatican copies (Inc. IV.662) does have it.

24. See Bühler, *The Fifteenth-Century Book,* pp. 163-164.

## An Unusual Educational Device of Aldus Manutius

1. See *Aldi Institutionum grammaticarum libri quatuor* (1508), Literarii ludi magistris.

2. See *Aldus Mannuccius Bassianas Latinus Catharinae Piae claris-simae ac prudentissimae* in *Aldi Pii Manutii, Scripta tria longe rarissima a Jacobo Morellio denuo edita et illustrata* (Bassani, 1806), p. 8.

3. *Musarum Panagyris* printed in Morelli, *Scripta tria,* pp. 1-5. It was Prince Alberto who later subsidized Aldus' edition of Aristotle's works. In his will, Aldus asked to be buried on the Carpi estate.

4. *Paranesis* in Morelli, *Scripta tria,* p. 6-7.

5. See *Epistola* in Morelli, *Scripta tria,* pp. 10-13.

6. This statement was first made in Aldus' 1494-95 edition of Lascaris' Greek grammar in the preface to the Appendix. It was used later in other editions of the Greek grammar and also of the Latin grammar.

7. The 1501 edition was entitled *Rudimenta grammaticae Latinae linguae.* It is extremely rare and I have not seen a copy of it. My remarks are based on the second edition of 1508 which is a reprinting of the 1501 work. Copies of all the other Aldine books here mentioned are in the Beinecke Library.

8. "Malo enim eos nullas scire literas ornatos moribus, quam omnia scire male moratos."

9. There are very few exceptions. In several instances where he is giving lists of verbs, he does give the equivalents in Italian.

10. One such reference occurs in quire ii^v where he is discussing *syllepsis.* He says, "Dices per syllepsin Ferdinandus Rex et Elizabeth Regina Hispaniae homines qui iustissimi Bethycam, quae Granata numc dicitur, urbem et maximam et munitissimam et bellicosissimam opulen-tissimamque decem ab his annos obsessam et nunquam antea a Christianis debellatam, atque ideo summis laudibus, summoque honore dignissimi Anno a nativitate Iesu Christi Dei Opt. Max. millesimo quadringentesimo nonagesimo secundo, quarto Nonas Ianuarias expugnaverunt."

11. "In quarto libro, praeter ea quae connumerantur in fronte primi libri, habentur et haec: De pedibus in metro CXXIIII graece et latine."

12. The Latin translation is that of Giovanni Crastoni.

13. In the preface Aldus says that Constantinus Lascaris himself corrected the Greek text in over 150 instances before it was printed.

14. In a dedicatory epistle to Angelo Gabriele, Aldus pays tribute to Lascaris, the "father of Greek letters." and expresses his deep regret that he had not lived to see the second and third books of his grammar in print. Aldus' first edition of the Tragedies of Sophocles (1502) is dedicated to Lascaris.

15. In his preface to the reader he says, "Si forte nescieris, studiose lector, quonam modo quae graece imprimenda curavimus cum interpretatione latina ordinande sint ut pagina paginae respondeat et versus versui, utpote qui videas separatos quinterniones graecos ab iis qui latinam ipsorum continent tralationem, sic accipe posse te pro arbitrio tuo latinum graeco insertare, et ex duobus quinternionibus unum, et ex uno duos facere, si prius tamen adverteris ut latina pagina semper graecae opponatur. . . . Cum vero curavimus ut latinum a graeco separai queat, non te fugiat a nobis ob id factum ut et doctis qui nullo egent adiumento legendis graecis, et graecarum litterarum rudibus, qui nisi latinum e regione in graecis operibus viderint, a graecorum librorum lectione deterrentur, satisfaceremus."

16. "Aldus lectori S. Et quia binae eae, quae in singulorum quinternionum medio sitae sunt paginae abundabant, quoniam nullas habeant oppositas graecas quas latinae ostenderent, operae pretium duximus aliquid graece lectu dignum cum latino e regione in ipsis, ne perirent, imprimendum curare."

17. The translation of the Cebes text has not been identified. The German humanist, Johannes Aesticampianus, made an edition of the work in the same translation that was published in Frankfort in 1507.

18. "Parce igitur, carissime Lector, quoties erratum quid vides sis quia aequus iudex tantorum laborum quamque veniet spero tempus, idque brevi, quo decies et ad unguem castigatos suppeditemus libros studiosis. Nunc quamdiu argentea atque aurea vasa defuerint, samiis, ut aiunt, delectemur."

19. His graphic description of his extreme busyness is climaxed in his statement: "Interdum ita distinemur, utraque occupata manu atque coram expectantibus impressoribus . . . ut ne nasum quidem liceat emungere."

20. In a special note to the reader, Aldus says that translating these treatises was a Herculean task, but because he had promised to do it, and because it would be most useful to students, he would not evade his responsibility.

21. It is interesting to note that the edition of Lascaris' grammar published by Albus' successors in 1557 is printed in the conventional way and the Cebes text is included after the grammar (pp. 370-388).

22. Here, too, in a preface to the reader, Aldus again explains at length his method of arranging the texts and his reason for using the center fold for an unrelated text.

23. The preface to the second volume echoes these sentiments, but in a more vivid way as he says, "Nam sanctissimos libros, qui circiter mille annos latuere, publicavimus ut amentur, legantur in scholiis, fiatque non ut antehac cum fabulae, quibus tenera puerorum aetas imbuitur, pro historia habebantur, quae est potissima, ut puto, causa quia quamplurimum e doctis et vitiosi sunt et infideles."

24. A. A. Renouard (*Annales de l'imprimerie des Aldes*, Paris, 1825, I.109) feels that this device, over which Aldus took such pains, was not a success. He says, "On est désagreablement surpris de trouver deux pages de l'évangile de S. Jean à travers une pièce de poésie."

25. Renouard (*Annales* I. 117-119) describes the composition of this volume.

26. A Firmin-Didot (*Alde Manuce et l'Hellénisme à Venise*, Paris, 1875, p.iv) says, "Il fut critique, philologue, grammairien, historien de la litterature, moraliste, et il contribua pour une très-large part, par son initiative et ses travaux multiples, à la renaissance des lettres."

# Original Printing of Essays

# LIST OF MANUSCRIPTS CONSULTED
(All in Beinecke Library, Yale University)

MS 516
St. Gregory, *Moralia* (fragment) pp. 20-23

Marston MS 151
Paulus Diaconus, *Homiliarium* pp. 25-27

MS 484. no. 6
*Sacramentarium Gregorianum* (fragment) pp. 33-38

MS 513
Theodulus, *Ecologa*; Avianus, *Fabulae*; Maximianus, *Elegiae* pp. 42-45

MS 237
Johannes Climacus, *Scala Paradisi* pp. 48-49

Marston MS 80
Walter Burley, *De vita et moribus philosophorum*, with works of other authors p. 53

Marston MS 91
Walter Burley, *De vita et moribus philosophorum*, with treatise of Maphaeus Vegius p. 53

Marston MS 114
Walter Burley, *De vita et moribus philosophorum*, Italian translation p. 53

Marston MS 252
*Epistola Abgari ad Ihesum*, in manuscript of Gautier de Chatillon, *Gesta Alexandri Magni* pp. 61-62

MS 335
Nicholas Oresme, *Tractatus sperae*, with Johannes de Sacro Bosco, *De sphera* pp. 64, 68

MS 532
St. Basil of Caesarea, *De legendis gentilium libris*, bound with numerous Greek works on grammar and rhetoric pp. 75-76

MS 179
St. Basil of Caesarea, *De legendis gentilium libris*, Latin translation of Leonardo Bruni p. 75

Marston MS 105
St. Basil of Caesarea, *De legendis gentilium libris*, Latin translation of Leonardo Bruni, with other works p. 76

Marston MS 78
Plato, *Phaedo*, Latin translation of Leonardo Bruni, with Xenophon, *Hiero* p. 77

MS 207
St. Thomas Aquinas, *In Tertiam Sententiarum Petri Lombardi*
p. 132

MS 321
Poggio-Bracciolini, *Historia Florentina*, Italian translation of
Jacopo Poggio-Bracciolini p. 133

Zi +2093
Cicero, *Pro Marcello*, with two treatises in manuscript and
four incunabula p. 133

Zi.i6937.6
Pius II, *Carmen Sapphicum*, with five incunabula p. 134

MS 451
Johannes Antonius Campanus, Johannes de Margarit, Franciscus de Toleto, *Orationes* pp. 134-135

MS 508
*Foedus Edouardi et Guthruni regum* and *Leges Edouardi
regis*, with *Annals of Iceland* p. 135

MS 534
Musaeus, *Opusculum de Herone et Leandro* pp. 135-138


## LIST OF EARLY BOOKS CONSULTED
(All in Beinecke Library, Yale University, except as designated)

*Homiliarium doctorum*
Nuremberg, 1494 p. 25

Johannes Climacus, *Scala Paradisi*, Latin translation of Ambrogio
Traversari
Cologne, 1583 p. 49

Walter Burley, *De vita et moribus philosophorum*
Cologne, 1470 p. 53

Walter Burley, *De vita et moribus philosophorum*
Nuremberg, 1477 p. 53

Walter Burley, *De vita et moribus philosophorum*, German translation
Augsburg, 1490

Walter Burley (here called Diogenes Laertius), *De vita et moribus
philosophorum*, Italian translation
Venice, 1535 p. 53

Aesticampianus, edition of Cebes' *Tabula*
Leipzig, 1512 p. 79

Aesticampianus, edition of Martianus Capella, *De Grammatica*
  Frankfort, 1507
  (Universitätsbibliothek, Munich) pp. 79, 88
Aesticampianus, *Commentarii in De Grammatica Martiani Capel-
  lae* Frankfort, 1508
  (Sächsische Landesbibliothek, Dresden) pp. 88-95
Dubravius, *A New Book of Good Husbandry*
  London, 1599 pp. 99-102, 106
Dubravius, *Martianus Capella . . . cum Adnotationibus*
  Vienna, 1516 pp. 106-108, 110-111
Dubravius, *Theriobulia*
  Nuremberg, 1520
  (Houghton Library, Harvard University) pp. 114-120
Poggio-Bracciolini, *Historia Florentina*
  Venice, 1475 p. 133
Johannes Antonius Campanus, *Oratio*
  Rome, 1487 p. 134
Franciscus de Toleto, *Oratio*
  Rome, 1481-1487 p. 135
William Lambarde, APXAINOMIA
  London, 1568 p. 135
Musaeus, *Opusculum de Herone et Leandro*
  Florence, 1494 p. 136
  Venice, 1494-5 p. 136
  Paris, 1515 p. 136
  Venice, 1517 p. 137
Constantinus Lascaris, *Erotemata*
  Venice, 1494-5 p. 143
  Venice, 1501-2 p. 143
  Venice, 1512 p. 145
Aldus Pius Manutius, *Institutionum grammaticarum libri quatuor*
  Venice, 1508 pp. 140-144
Aldus Pius Manutius, *Poetae Christiani veteres*
  Venice, 1501-1504 pp. 145-146
Aldus Pius Manutius, *Grammaticae institutiones Graecae*
  Venice, 1515 p. 148
Aesopus, *Fabulae*
  Venice, 1505 p. 147
Pindarus, *Opera*
  Venice, 1515 p. 147

# INDEX

Abgarus V, Uchomo, King of Edessa, 57-58; Abgarus-Jesus Epistles, 57-58, 60-62

*Accessus ad auctores*, extols Maximianus' *Elegiae*, 44

Acciaiuoli, Niccolò, Petrarch's *De principis officio* dedicated to, 125

Aelfric, *Lives of the Saints*, 60

Aesop, *Fabulae*, 42, 147

Aesticampianus, Johannes Rhagius, 82-83, 95-96; *Tabula* of Cebes, 79, 82, 84-85; Commentary on Martianus Capella, 88, 90-94

Aetheria, *Peregrinatio*, 58

Alcuin, adds to *Homiliarium*, 34

Alexander VI, Pope, crowns Aesticampianus poet laureate, 83, 95

Alexandre de Villedieu, *Doctrinale*, 42, 45, 139

Alfonso of Calabria, Pontano's *Liber de principe* dedicated to, 125

Ananias, messenger of Abgarus, 57

Anastasius a Sala, plagiarizes Burley's *De vita et moribus philosophorum*, 51

Andrews, William L., donor to Yale, 136

Angelus de Cingulo, translates Climacus' *Scala Paradisi*, 49

Aristippus, quoted, 56

Aristotle, *De caelo et mundo*, 67; *Politica, Ethica, Oeconomica*, 69

Augustinus, St., Bishop of Hippo, 54; *De doctrina Christiana*, 73; *Confessiones*, 74

Augustine, St., missionary to England, 19-20

Avianus, *Fabulae*, 42-43

Babrius (Gabrias), *Fabulae*, 44, 47

Baptista di Montefeltre, Bruni's *De legendis gentilium libris* dedicated to, 76

Basil of Caesaria, St., *Address*, 74-78

Bede, The Venerable, 23; *Ecclesiastical History*, 19-20, 22; *Sermons*, 25-26

Behaim, Martin, 'Erdapfel', 66

Beinecke, Edwin J., legacy to Yale, 42

Benedict, Abbot of Monte Cassino, helps compile *Homiliarium*, 24

Benedict Biscop, Abbot of Wearmouth and Jarrow, 22

Bernard of Clairvaux, St., *Scala Paradisi*, 47

Bernard of Utrecht, Commentary on *Ecloga* of Theodulus, 43

Berners, Dame Juliana, *On Fishing with an Angle*, 102

Beroaldus, Philip, teaches Aesticampianus, 83, 95-96; edits Cebes' *Tabula*, 82

Boethius, related to Maximianus, 44; source for Burley, 54

Boniface, St., quoted, 23

Bruni, Leonardo, translates St. Basil's *De legendis gentilium libris*, 76; translates *Phaedo*, 77

Burley, Walter, 51, 56; *De vita et moribus philosophorum*, 51-56

Burton, Robert, cites Dubravius' *On Fishponds*, 103

Busche, Herman von dem, German humanist, 96

Calliergus, Z., publishes Cebes' *Tabula*, 82

Campanus, Johannes Antonius, Bishop of Teramo, *Oratio*, 134

Carpi, Alberto, pupil of Aldus, 140

Carpi, Leonello, pupil of Aldus, 140

Casimir IV, King of Poland, 116

Castiglione, Baldassare, *Il Cortegiano*, 125

Cato, *Disticha Catonis*, 41-42

Caxton, William, *Golden Legend*, 61

Cebes, author of *Tabula*, 79-80, 144